The Wilderness Within

Exploring Women's Spiritual Struggles

BENETH PETERS JONES

JOURNEYFORTH

Greenville, South Carolina

Library of Congress Cataloging-in-Publication Data

Jones, Beneth Peters, 1937-
The wilderness within : exploring women's spiritual struggles / Beneth Peters Jones.
   p. cm.
   ISBN 1-57924-819-5 (pbk. : alk. paper)
   1. Christian women—Religious life. 2. Emotions—Religious aspects—Christianity. 3. Attitude (Psychology)—Religious aspects—Christianity.
I. Title.
   BV4527 .J674 2002
   248.8'43—dc21

                                                          2002003780

Cover image by PhotoDisc, Inc.

All Scripture is quoted from the Authorized King James Version.

The Wilderness Within: Exploring Women's Spiritual Struggles

Design by Jamie Leong
Page layout by Jennifer Hearing

© 2002 by BJU Press
Greenville, South Carolina 29614
JourneyForth Books is an imprint of BJU Press   .

Printed in the United States of America

ISBN 978-1-57924-819-2

15 14 13 12 11 10 9 8 7 6 5 4 3 2

To the dear folks at Camp Ironwood
and Wilderness Tracks,
who graciously afforded opportunity
for real progress on this
WOMAN'S WILDERNESS
manuscript

$\mathscr{T}$ABLE OF CONTENTS

PREFACE

"Writing is hard work." How many times I've spoken those words in reply to a starry-eyed someone desiring publication. But *The Wilderness Within* has proven that truth to the *n*th degree.

The *labor* of writing was no surprise; as usual, page after page of manuscript went into the wastebasket. But for this book the *battle* of writing reached the intensity of all-out warfare. There is no adequate description for my constant sense of satanic opposition. Bombardment has been intense and furious in every area: ministry . . . marriage . . . interpersonal relationships . . . technological production . . . spiritual sustenance . . . physical well-being . . . and mental clarity.

Time after time, however, just when the entire *Wilderness* project was about to be abandoned, God intervened. Women would ask if there were another book on the way; when told the topic of attitudes and emotions, they brightened, saying something to this effect: "Oh— please get that finished *soon*. How I need it!" Masculine comments, too, invariably urged me forward. At one point, a young man said, "Let my wife proofread that, okay?" And an older man in the group added, "*Every* woman could proofread a manuscript on that topic!"

Can any Christian woman be unaware that her attitudes and emotions represent her greatest spiritual vulnerability? The *internal* woman is Satan's focus; he unceasingly works against each of us in that wilderness landscape. No wonder, then, his opposition to this manuscript.

I want to assure you before you begin that there will be no page on which I'll stand apart on some comfortable spiritual oasis "preaching" at you out there in wilderness struggles. Instead, I believe that the best way—indeed the only way—to reach and help another woman's inner self is to reveal my own. As my innumerable wilderness failures become evident, a reader can (a) acknowledge her own foibles, (b) recognize Satan's lie that she's uniquely horrible and hopeless, and (c) allow me to come alongside her so that we can move together toward the challenge and help of God's Word, the Bible.

Here at last, then, is the completed book. It comes bathed in my prayer that God may use it in some small way to edify you and to exalt Him.

In His love—and mine,

Beneth Peters Jones

Part One

SURVEYING
THE
Wilderness

THE
Wilderness
ITSELF

He found him in a desert land, and in the waste howling wilderness; he led him about, he instructed him, he kept him as the apple of his eye.
Deuteronomy 32:10

DISCOVERING THE WILDERNESS

Welcome to some challenging territory: the wilderness
of feminine attitudes and emotions. This poorly charted
landscape can sometimes resemble the Sahara's heat, the
Negev's barrenness, and the Gobi's extensiveness all in one!

What are attitudes and emotions, anyway? My *American
Heritage Dictionary* defines them quite simply:

> ✎ Attitude—a mental position or disposition; a
>   mindset that strongly influences behavior.

> ✎ Emotion—any specific feeling; a complex reaction
>   involving both physical and mental response.

The simplicity of these definitions, however, vanishes
in the chasm that lies between *definition* and *demonstration*.

The wilderness of our emotions and attitudes demonstrates its presence, its vastness, and its influence in and
through all feminine human beings. Masculine beings of
course have attitudes and emotions, too; however, in them
the territory is far less fearsome.

Whether or not you have ever likened your internal
non-physical workings to a wilderness, you undoubtedly

have puzzled over, agonized in, and felt overwhelmed by the reality and power of those workings. My purpose in writing this book is to demystify the territory and benefit our sojourn therein.

My own inner wilderness first became evident at the age of twelve. Interestingly, external and internal wildernesses appeared simultaneously.

Prior to seventh grade, our branch of the Peters family lived in Washington State. What an idyllic setting for childhood! A tiny Norwegian community nestled on Puget Sound wrapped my first six years of life in the sights, sounds, and scents of saltwater beaches, towering evergreens, gently flowing creeks, and carpeting wildflowers. I attended school through first and second grades in a two-room country schoolhouse, which served all local children below high school age. Then my father moved us east of the Cascades to a small riverside town in apple-growing country. There I reveled in the sweep of rolling open spaces, fragrant fruit orchards, warm summers, and snowy winters. There, too, special friendships blossomed, and several of those friends gave me access to my dream animals: horses. Not only did I love to be around and ride horses, I wanted *to be* one. Enabled by a vivid imagination, I was transformed almost daily into a splendid steed—galloping, jumping, snorting, and neighing. Ah, the fun and freedom of it all.

Then came seventh grade. We moved again—this time to Phoenix, Arizona. It would be difficult to find any place more unlike Washington State. The stark contrasts were evident everywhere. We left lush, restful country panoramas for blazing barrenness and the frenetic pace of a city. I was set down smack in the middle of what I considered a physical wilderness. But the negative realities of Phoenix were only part of the whole. The timing of our move was also a critical factor: seventh grade.

Junior high school: do you remember it? For me, it was the epitome of *awful*. Childhood's cocoon suddenly burst and a changed creature emerged—a complicated, newly configured, and wholly contradictory being. My physical awkwardness somehow created internal slumping and stumbling, too—and all that amid schoolmates who were prone to ridicule rather than encourage, to shun rather than include. There was also the added difficulty of transferring to a strange school—not just once, but several times before Daddy decided on the area of town he preferred.

So it was that the geographical area I considered wilderness was reflected inside me: my own invisible Badlands. I endured bleak stretches of self-pity, resentment, disappointment, anger, depression, complaint, and many subtle or vivid variations thereof.

Arizona and age twelve are both far behind me now. Yet even as a grandmother my internal wilderness of attitudes and emotions is very real. That challenging expanse has nothing to do with geography, or age, but everything to do with womanhood.

For you a woman reader, then, I ask you to come with me on an exploratory journey. Without even leaving your chair we can, together, travel far and discover much.

The Starting Point

Let's begin this exploration by seeking to understand the start of all wildernesses—both the geographical and personal.

The earth's face is pockmarked with wilderness areas large and small. Human civilization sprouts and flourishes on the hospitable sections of the globe, but it struggles in or avoids wilderness regions.

Why does such harshness encroach upon the earth's more pleasant surface? To answer that question, we must go back to Genesis. There we find that our planet was intended and created by God as a wholly beautiful place. Looking upon His newly molded sphere of earth, God pronounced that it was—all—"good."

> *And God saw every thing that he had made, and, behold, it was very good. And the evening and the morning were the sixth day (Genesis 1:31).*

The thoroughgoing beauty of earth in her virginity is hard to imagine today, for her ruin lies between that time and ours. The freshness of creation saw a lovely interim when man and woman walked in perfect fellowship with God and with each other amid Eden's lushness. But the hands on Time's clock had barely begun to move before the Destroyer emerged from the shadows. Interestingly, a question posed in Isaiah 14:16-17 identifies this one as follows:

> *Is this the man . . . that made the world as a wilderness?*

"This man"—Satan—made a tragic advance in his battle against God there in Eden's verdure. The effect upon nature was dramatic. The lush, nurturing beauty of God's garden gave way to Satan's barren wilderness of sin. Where once all had been life and health, universal suffering and death entered. Multihued green was decimated by monotonous, lifeless drab. Henceforth, the earth's surface would yield her fruits to mankind only at the price of his endless toil. On and on until the great Creator cries "Done!" must the earth whirl sadly on its way, bearing its many wilderness scars.

As in forming the earth, so too in creating male and female, God's creation was good. When the first woman, Eve, hearkened to the Serpent's lies and led her husband Adam into sin, the results were devastating not only to the physical world around her but also to the world *within* her. Both became a wilderness simultaneously. So it is that throughout our earthly sojourn as daughters of Eve we experience the harshness of an internal wilderness.

When God pronounced His chastisement upon man and woman for their sin, He focused on different aspects of their being:

> *Unto the woman he said, I will greatly multiply thy sorrow and thy conception; in sorrow thou shalt bring forth children; and thy desire shall be to thy husband, and he shall rule over thee. And unto Adam he said, Because thou has hearkened unto the voice of thy wife, and hast eaten of the tree, of which I commanded thee, saying, Thou shalt not eat of it: cursed is the ground for thy sake; in sorrow shalt thou eat of it all the days of thy life; thorns also and thistles shall it bring forth to thee; and thou shalt eat the herb of the field; in the sweat of thy face shalt thou eat bread, till thou return unto the ground* (Genesis 3:16-19).

Sin's intrusion made woman's suffering primarily inward, centering in heart and soul. First, "sorrow" and "conception" are linked—the greatest womanly fulfillment was to be accompanied by expanded suffering. Second, she would suffer in her primary human relationship: marriage.

> And thy desire shall be to thy husband, and he
> shall rule over thee (Genesis 3:16).

Bible commentators differ as to the precise meaning of God's pronouncement here, but it is clear that sin's scar upon woman's inner self would adversely affect the marriage relationship.

By contrast, man's suffering was to be more external and physical: he would know unending physical toil in order to exist in the sin-mangled world.

Driven out from the Garden of Eden, Adam and Eve began their disastrously changed existence in a scarred physical world. We men and women today must continue to occupy and struggle in that same setting until God at last creates a new heaven and a new earth. In our wilderness world, we long for the fulfillment of the apostle John's vision:

> And I saw a new heaven and a new earth: for
> the first heaven and the first earth were passed away;
> and there was no more sea (Revelation 21:1).

Meanwhile, our great archenemy, Satan, holds sway as the god of this world. He is Apollyon—the Destroyer—he delights in and battles to maintain the wilderness he has made, both external and internal.

Satanic efforts against our inner self actually reveal to us the intrinsic value of the area! God's creation is a *good* creation, howbeit now sin flawed. Lest we be discouraged at the outset of our exploratory journey, I want to establish

the positives of feminine inner workings. We need always
to remember that they are God's handiwork.

Without our inner structure and functioning, our fe-
maleness would be incomplete. Our mental and emotional
capacity does inwardly what hormones and bone structure
do outwardly: they "round our edges," giving the soft curves
that make us and mark us.

Woman is a nurturer, a self-investor. That approach to
life demands a source from which withdrawals are made.
Her emotional self provides the source. Much like a water
reservoir, its outflow is compensated by intake: perceived
need for what she provides.

One of woman's most strategic roles as helper to man is
that of nurturing—not only by gestating life but also by
protecting and encouraging life that already exists. In order
to do the latter, she must be capable of being reached by
the plight of others. It is her emotional self that both senses
needs and responds to them.

Isn't it interesting that when new life is created by the
coming together of husband and wife, the life-giving
essence is projected *out* of man but comes *in* to woman;
moreover, the newly created life is not carried externally
to its moment of birth, but rather internally. That natal
preparation and process is echoed throughout a woman's
life in her daily experiences. As our children have grown
up, married, and begun their own families, my husband's
primary interest and concern is for their "externals"—job
satisfaction, financial health, and so forth. Mine is more
for their "internals" such as response to pressures and
hurts, personal relationships. . . .

Mental and emotional warmth is active throughout a
woman's waking hours in her personal relationships and is

as much a part of her life as breathing. Those human beings given into her care, whether by marriage, birth, family
ties, or professional relationships, draw from her not just
intellectual interest but emotional identification. Man
lives *among* people at the various levels of contact, woman
lives *with* them: she reaches into their core selves through
concern and draws them into her own with compassion.
For instance, she listens to her husband's or roommate's
or close friend's tales of difficulties in the workplace and
responds not so much from an intellectual or practical
standpoint as from an emotionally vicarious one—she re-
acts from *within*, and she extends comfort and encouragement to the one confiding in her.

Woman responds to life's experiences by *internalizing*
them. That is, they do not speak primarily to her practical
intellect but rather to her receptive heart and her percep-
tive mind.

The Bible phrase "fearfully and wonderfully made"
certainly applies to the human brain. Its marvels far exceed
the most advanced computer man has ever or will ever de-
vise. The ability to *think* is uniquely human, and our mental
processes are fascinating. God designed the human brain—
our operations center—with two halves, or lobes: a left and
a right. While man is primarily left-brained, woman operates mostly from the right lobe. She processes multiple foci
and has more connectors between the right brain and the
left, integrating the lesser-used half into her thought
processes quite freely. There are also other gender-related
characteristics of our feminine mental operation: introspec-
tion, sensitivity, subjectivity, and multifocus.

The Personal Challenge

Twenty-first century America presents a three-dimensional picture of satanic assault upon woman's internal self. We're told that innate femininity does not exist, that it is a confining costume forced upon us by negative society mores. We're urged to be brash, brassy, and self-seeking. We're told not to complement masculinity but to compete with it. We're harangued with claims that marriage and child-rearing are forms of enslavement. We're inundated through print, film, broadcast, and Internet with reminders of our "rights"—whether it means sexual impurity, murder of the unborn, or whatever. Laughably incongruous is the fact that while much of the barrage seeks to destroy the concept of our female emotional nature, the whole tone of the barrage itself is blatantly emotional.

While the spirit of our nation obviously reflects its ungodly majority population, it nevertheless illustrates the dangers of human internal wilderness left unopposed.

A born-again Christian is instructed by Scripture to be different from those who "know not God." The difference is not merely a matter of external, observable factors but of our internal selves as well. The natural tendencies of our private inner wilderness, then, must not only be recognized but must also be resisted. The Bible makes it plain that our private struggles are important in God's eyes:

> *The spirit of man is the candle of the Lord,*
> *searching all the inward parts of the belly (Proverbs*
> *20:27).*
> *He that hath no rule over his own spirit is like a*
> *city that is broken down, and without walls (Proverbs*
> *25:28).*

So there it lies: a great internal expanse known as attitudes and emotions. We have seen that it is part of God's good creation. We've noted how integral it is to our feminine makeup. We've recognized Satan at work in the area—both initially in Eden and in his intensifying determination to worsen its barrenness.

Now let's move on to explore the area together. Although we will survey the landscape and examine various places along the way, our heart focus will be upward. We will move forward strengthened by three spiritual facts: our all-wise God originally designed femininity's internal landscape as a garden, He knows exactly how and where Satan has decimated it, and He can equip us for successful travels therein.

There are many ways to approach the wilderness of our feminine attitudes and emotions. Trying to define or chart "feelings" is like trying to collect water in a sieve. So I'm going to use parallelism: the real people and their experiences found in the Book of Exodus will illuminate and illustrate our inner self.

When I was a child, the Old Testament seemed difficult and the characters who peopled its pages so remote they appeared alien to human experience. My mother, though, urged me to include the Old Testament in all my Bible reading and study. How thankful I am! As years have passed, my study of God's recorded working prior to His sending the Messiah has been a major contributor to my personal soul growth. Its dear, familiar pages have let me glimpse the faces of real people from the past while simultaneously revealing my own face in the present.

Years of studying those pages yield increasingly personal and powerful lessons. Christians are not left to conduct their lives in a hit-or-miss fashion: God gives us the Bible. In it He clearly instructs us, and He tells us that by obeying His Word we demonstrate the reality and the quality of our love for Him:

> If ye love me, keep my commandments (John 14:15).
>
> Ye are my friends, if ye do whatsoever I command you (John 15:14).

The practical living out of our faith is hard. The difficulty is not in the nature of the instruction but in the nature of the student. You and I are so weak in our humanity that we find it difficult to comprehend and personalize God's instructions for living. Knowing our frailty, the Lord doesn't just repeat His instructions; He also illustrates. Those illustrations are wonderfully helpful. They serve as object lessons that enable us to grasp concepts—as translators that put the immensity of God's mind into the alphabet of personal reality. So it is in the story of Israel's travels to Canaan.

As we prepare to study the object lesson of Israel's journeys, let me establish the exact way in which we can parallel our life and theirs.

The Wilderness

- Theirs was a physical, geographical expanse. They experienced sand, and heat, and parching thirst. The area can be seen on a globe.

- Ours is the inner self of mind and emotions. We experience the grit of negative thought processes, the rising temperature of emotional pressures, and the mirages of unfulfilled yearnings.

The Campsites

> 🌿 Theirs were points that can be located on a map. Your personal Bible probably has a page tracing their journey.

> 🌿 Ours are the circumstances and experiences of life. Whether we stay briefly or long, each "encampment" affects us and we respond to it.

Whether actual or internal, the wilderness was/is inescapable reality; the *responses* throughout are *human choices*.

We need to recognize at the outset of our exploration that our internal wilderness is a place of distinctive opportunity for God's operation. Our heavenly Father wants it to be *a place of learning and of love*. At present we must move forward in faith; but one day in the future we'll see that our wilderness times, like Israel's long ago, have purpose:

> *To humble thee, and to prove thee, to know what was in thine heart, whether thou wouldest keep his commandments, or no (Deuteronomy 8:2).*

The proving and the heart-knowing of which God speaks are not for the sake of *His* understanding, but for *ours*. Our Creator knows us intimately and totally. Our self-knowledge, however, is pathetically sketchy and inaccurate. God states the case this way:

> *The heart is deceitful above all things, and desperately wicked: who can know it? (Jeremiah 17:9).*

Our unlovely heart condition becomes apparent to us only as we respond to life's circumstances.

Genuine self-knowledge, however unflattering, is an important part of the growing Christian life. Scripture urges the believer to change—to grow toward Christlikeness. Points of self-revelation are like marks on a gauge: they indicate our spiritual position and progress.

But wilderness—a place of learning and of love? God's Word repeatedly assures us that our places of overwhelming are His places of undertaking.

THE

Wilderness
WANDERER

*Yet I am the Lord thy God from the land of Egypt,
and thou shalt know no god but me:
for there is no saviour beside me.
I did know thee in the wilderness, in the land of
great drought.
Hosea 13:4-5*

ENTERING THE WILDERNESS

Exodus. The long, tortuous pilgrimage of Israel's vast throng was in itself a marvel: the original "cast of thousands." But the throng was made up of people—individual human beings like you and me. There is much we can learn from them. Of course that is God's intention. He tells us:

> *Now all these things happened unto them for ensamples: and they are written for our admonition, upon whom the ends of the world are come (I Corinthians 10:11).*

Those who would go to Canaan, the Promised Land, had to do two things:

2. escape death.

2. leave Egypt.

There was only one way to accomplish them: God's way. The people had to obey His instructions and step out in faith.

The beginning of Israel's journey was a corporate and physical one; the beginning of ours is individual and spiritual. The one beautifully illustrates the other.

God inflicted plague after plague upon Egypt to persuade Pharaoh to let the Israelites leave the country. Still, the king refused to release those whose slave labors were so important to him. Finally, Jehovah sent the angel of death to sweep through the land: every household would lose its firstborn. There was only one means of escaping death: an unblemished lamb had to be slain for each family, its blood used to mark the home's doorway.

> And they shall take of the blood, and strike it on the two side posts and on the upper door post of the houses (Exodus 12:7).
> And the blood shall be to you for a token upon the houses where ye are: and when I see the blood, I will pass over you (Exodus 12:13).

So begins the drama of Exodus. The journey of an individual's soul is likewise dramatic. God deals very directly and personally.

Long ago there in Egypt, physical death threatened the Israelites. Today, spiritual death threatens every individual born into the world. The judgment of death (eternal separation from God in hell) has been pronounced upon each individual because God, who is holy, will not dwell with sin:

> Your iniquities have separated between you and your God (Isaiah 59:2).
> As it is written, There is none righteous, no, not one (Romans 3:10).
> For all have sinned, and come short of the glory of God (Romans 3:23).

*For the wages of sin is death; but the gift of God
is eternal life through Jesus Christ our Lord (Romans
6:23).*

As for Israel, so for you and me—only the life's blood
of a substitute turns aside God's condemnation:

*Behold the Lamb of God, which taketh away the
sin of the world (John 1:29).*
*But God commendeth His love toward us, in
that, while we were yet sinners, Christ died for us
(Romans 5:8).*
*There is one God, and one mediator between God
and men, the man Christ Jesus (I Timothy 2:5).*
*For He [God the Father] hath made him [Christ
the Son] to be sin for us, who knew no sin; that we
might be made the righteousness of God in him (II
Corinthians 5:21).*

In order to be safe from the angel of death, the Israelites
had to be *inside* the blood-marked doorway. They had to accept God's plan by faith. So must you and I. The Lord Jesus
Christ is both the Lamb, whose blood saves us from death,
and the Door through which we enter into eternal life:

*I am the door: by me if any man enter in, he
shall be saved (John 10:9).*
*In whom we have redemption through his blood,
the forgiveness of sins, according to the riches of his
grace (Ephesians 1:7).*
*Verily, verily, I say unto you, He that heareth
my word, and believeth on him that sent me, hath
everlasting life, and shall not come into condemnation; but is passed from death unto life (John 5:24).*

He that believeth on the Son hath everlasting life:
and he that believeth not the Son shall not see life; but
the wrath of God abideth on him (John 3:36).

And you, that were sometime alienated and ene-
mies in your mind by wicked works, yet now hath he
reconciled in the body of his flesh through death, to
present you holy and unblameable and unreproveable
in his sight (Colossians 1:21-22).

Having been spared the awful visitation by the angel
of death, the Israelites had another choice to make: the
choice to follow God's leading. They then left Egypt—the
land wherein they had been slaves:

And it came to pass at the end of the four hun-
dred and thirty years, even the selfsame day it came
to pass, that all the hosts of the Lord went out from
the land of Egypt (Exodus 12:41).

Having been delivered from God's eternal condemnation, you and I are to leave "Egypt"—the dark country of
sin wherein we were slaves:

Therefore, if any man be in Christ, he is a new
creature: old things are passed away; behold, all
things are become new (II Corinthians 5:17).

But now being made free from sin, and become
servants to God, ye have your fruit unto holiness,
and the end ever-lasting life (Romans 6:22).

What shall we say then? Shall we continue in sin,
that grace may abound? God forbid. How shall we,
that are dead to sin, live any longer therein? (Romans
6:1-2).

From the moment they left Egypt, the children of
Israel began moving toward the Promised Land—that lush,
nurturing place specially prepared and preserved for them:

> *Unto a good land, and a large, unto a land flow-
> ing with milk and honey (Exodus 3:8).*

From the moment an individual begins her new life in
Christ, she begins moving toward heaven—that marvelous
Eden of eternity:

> *In my Father's house are many mansions: if it
> were not so, I would have told you. I go to prepare a
> place for you (John 14:2).*
>
> *Eye hath not seen, nor ear heard, neither have en-
> tered into the heart of man, the things which God hath
> prepared for them that love Him (I Corinthians 2:9).*

The end of the journey for Israel was to be compara-
tively wonderful; the *way* of the journey—immediately
and throughout—was *wilderness*.

The end of our earthly life journey will be completely
wonderful; the *way* of our journey—immediately and
throughout—is *wilderness*. For the woman traveler, the
hardship is not that of a body suffering from the characteristics, creatures, and challenges of a physical wilderness but
of a soul struggling in her invisible, internal wilderness.

Having "come alongside" the newly released Israelites
by recognizing how we can identify with them, let's move
on with them now into wilderness travel.

First, there was apparently a gathering place to which
the Jews came from all parts of Egypt to become a unified
group.

*And the children of Israel journeyed from
Rameses to Succoth, about six hundred thousand on
foot that were men, beside children. And a mixed
multitude went up also with them; and flocks, and
herds, even very much cattle (Exodus 12:37-38).*

The word "Succoth" means "booths"—perhaps indicating temporary, rather flimsy structures to serve as shelters of sorts during the gathering process. We might consider our "Succoth" to be our local church: that physical place where we come together in the fellowship of believers—moving apart from the "Egypt" around us. We, of course, meet there regularly. There is great encouragement in knowing that we are not isolated but that others are making the journey with us.

Once the group was formed, they began the journey toward Canaan.

*And they took their journey from Succoth, and
encamped in Etham, in the edge of the wilderness
(Exodus 13:20).*

*And it came to pass, when Pharaoh had let the
people go, that God led them not through the way of
the land of the Philistines, although that was near
(Exodus 13:17).*

*But God led the people about, through the way of
the wilderness of the Red sea (Exodus 13:18).*

In this very first notation about Israel's introduction to the wilderness there are some thought-provoking considerations.

Although the Israelites had been rescued from slavery and death in Egypt, they were not instantly and miracu-

lously translated to Canaan; they had a long way to travel
and an unfriendly landscape through which to journey.

What did God's choice for Israel mean, exactly, in
human terms? It meant an indirect, extended, and difficult
route.

There they were, a great number of people unac-
quainted with the rigors of nomadic living (they'd been
settled in Egypt 430 years)—and God set them upon a
path that they themselves would not have chosen.

Isn't that essentially the story of our life journey? As
children we dream of "how things will be" in the land of
adulthood. We plan and prepare for the dream's fulfillment. Ultimately, however, God redirects us according to
His plans:

> A man's heart deviseth his way: but the Lord
> directeth his steps (Proverbs 16:9).

We often learn that our route is

- indirect (But why must I go by way of "7" to get
  from "A" to "B"?).

- long (Shouldn't spiritual maturity be an instant
  "zap"?).

- and difficult (My "narrow" way is a steep way
  too!).

However, when the pathway proves to be unrecognizable as
that one designed by our heart, we can glean tremendous
encouragement from a phrase in our text that explains
God's choice. The route chosen was

> not through the way of the land of the Philistines,
> although that was near (Exodus 13:17).

Looking down from above, our all-wise heavenly Father gauges the comparative dangers of routing. The wilderness holds not only its own inherent difficulties but also enemies poised for attack along the way. He knows if and when we are ready to face Satan's Green Berets. When in heaven, where we shall "know as we are known," the pathway puzzles will become clear, and we'll understand how God protected us time after time.

Such detours appear frequently along the road of life. Some are major, others minor. Interestingly, the Israelites accepted their first major reroute without a fuss. The newness of their freedom from Egypt made them compliant to Jehovah's routing. I blush to think of the times when even tiny pathway alterations have left me frustrated. So many have involved the "although that was near" aspect:

- a plane trip delayed or interrupted.

- a child's homecoming delayed by work demands.

- a speaking engagement derailed by laryngitis.

- a project shelved by interruptions.

In each instance, God's rebuke has reminded me that I'm simply to *follow*—not to figure out, and certainly not to fuss.

Another factor in the beginning phase of Israel's journey awakens empathy: when the people left Egypt, everything about their life became new and different. Yes, they had groaned for freedom and bewailed the harshness of slavery; nevertheless, there had been familiarity in their days. We human beings are creatures of habit; we draw security from that which is familiar; women particularly value that security, and we can be shaken by change. Therefore, Israel's struggles with those things that were new, different, strange, and challenging throughout their journey resonate with us.

Every change entails the end of something familiar and the start of something strange in that the new is *different*. Change points are many, and they run the gamut of type and impact. Whenever and wherever one occurs, it can raise the temperature in the wilderness! Consider just a few examples:

- Moving—
  across town
  from country to city
  to a foreign country
  from one church seating section to another
  repeatedly

- Loss—

  of independence
  by salvation
  by marriage
  by childbirth
  by physical debilitation

  of position
  by replacement
  by retirement

  of people
  by relocation
  by desertion
  by death

While there are rich lessons already available to us by this point on our parallel pathways, we are merely standing at the edge of the territory to be traversed. Much more lay ahead for Israel; much faces us as well. Here we first *see* the wilderness; from this point we go on to *settle into* our wilderness journey.

Israel first encamped *"in Etham in the edge of the wilderness."* The Hebrew word "Etham" is interesting: "a place in the desert." Although the differences between Egypt's splendor and the desert's severity were immediately evident to the eye, the newly dislodged people were buffered by God's keeping them at the *edge* of that vast expanse for a time. He does the same for us. In one very real sense, woman's internal wilderness first becomes reality at the time of puberty. What a jolt! Remember childhood's comfortable rhythm, the heedless passage of days? We were familiar with the territory, so to speak. Then, suddenly, came wilderness: the bewildering attitudinal and emotional expanses that accompanied a drastically changing body. Ah, but that was just the *edge* of the new territory, wasn't it? Although the rigors of puberty's upheavals were strange and challenging, we were buffered by the accompanying excitement of entering physical womanhood. We soon recognize, however, that we stand merely at the edge of ongoing body-connected wilderness struggles with attitudes and emotions.

Physical Influences

Because our physical structure and functioning tie in so strongly to our internal struggles, let's briefly review the points that apply. Although such a recap may seem overly elementary, it can instead solidify our understanding and thus contribute positively toward wilderness success.

Once past the transformational stage of puberty, man lives in a fairly stable physical state, chemically speaking.

How different that is from woman! For her, rather than being the one-time-around-and-then-shave-daily event of masculinity, puberty creates a monthly chemical roller coaster.

The mature female body is a *cyclical* body. That fact would have little significance if our Creator had seen fit to construct human beings in three distinct, separate compartments of body, mind, and spirit. Instead, He made us intricately *integrated:*

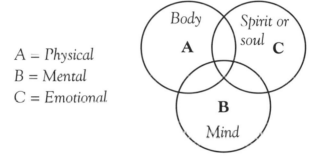

A = *Physical*
B = Mental
C = Emotional

When any one segment of our makeup experiences something, the other segments are also affected.

To illustrate our unified makeup, imagine pouring liquid dye into the physical circle (A) of the above diagram. The colorant does not affect the primary circle alone; it infuses the other two as well.

Chemical components make up the physical human body. God created Adam from the dust of the earth. When He pronounced sin's curse, He said, "Dust thou art, and unto dust shalt thou return." That is undeniably proven in death: the human body, minus its ever-living soul, gradually but surely turns to dust. We are not only chemical in construction, however; as living creatures, chemicals in our structure also affect the way we think and feel. And, conversely, our thoughts and feelings affect us chemically and physically.

A major element affecting women in physical and chemical terms is menstruation. Although it may seem unnecessary to deal with a matter as basic to womanhood as the menstrual cycle, I have seen women of all ages enlightened and helped by straightforward information on how the physical cycle can echo in mind and emotions. For any number of reasons, it is still possible for someone to grow through girlhood and well into maturity without ever having a clear picture of the kaleidoscopic biological and chemical changes within her own body.

As a woman goes through her monthly menstrual cycle, *actual chemical adjustments* occur due to hormonal activity. The major part of any month (thank the Lord!) finds us able to experience and respond to life's vicissitudes reasonably well. But there is a period of roughly seven to ten days that particularly invites wilderness struggles.

The most difficult phase of the monthly cycle is the premenstrual period. Medical researchers rather belatedly have discovered the many chemical-induced effects that may occur during those days; they are so distinguishable that the problem has been given a label: premenstrual syndrome. Symptoms may appear either singly or in clusters:

- fatigue

- backache and/or pelvic pain

- headaches

- hot flashes

- temperature change

- lowered sex drive

- physical clumsiness

- acne/blotching

- sweating

- bowel changes

- cravings for sweet or salty foods

- abdominal bloating

- swelling in hands and feet

- tender breasts

- anxiety/nervousness

- increased accidents and errors

- depression

- irritability

- confusion

- difficulty in concentrating/remembering

- tearfulness

Hardly a happy list, is it? Notice, especially, how the symptoms include physical, mental, and emotional manifestations. Moreover, symptoms may change from month to month, or an established pattern may make a drastic change. For instance, it is not uncommon for women who have been relatively symptom free up through their twenties suddenly to encounter intense symptomatic experiences in their thirties.

The fleeing Jews "encamped" in Etham. That is, they set up their tents—temporary dwellings. Right at the start of the wilderness experience it was clear that the forbidding territory *was not their permanent home*. We Christian women can similarly encourage ourselves. The Jews of Exodus were not all that thrilled with tent living, but the discomforts and bothers of their nomadic setting were in themselves reminders of their impermanence. So too, the difficulties we experience within these mortal bodies can likewise remind us that we are simply

strangers and pilgrims (I Peter 2:11)

in temporary dwellings. Throughout our earthly life we would do well to echo the apostle Peter:

Knowing that shortly I must put off this my tabernacle (II Peter 1:14).

Whether thirteen or ninety-three, God's woman wisely views her mortal "tenting" days in light of their impermanence.

Temporary! For Israel it meant temporary tents. Temporary dust, scorpions, heat, thirst, sandstorms. For you and me it means temporary physical challenges and limitations. Temporary attitude whirlwinds and emotional sandstorms. *All* of it is temporary!

But there was something even more marvelous in the wilderness at Etham: God demonstrated that He was there.

And the Lord went before them by day in a pillar of a cloud, to lead them the way; and by night in a pillar of fire, to give them light; to go by day and night: he took not away the pillar of the cloud by day, nor the pillar of fire by night, from before the people (Exodus 13:21-22).

It must be awful to face woman's wilderness struggles without an all-powerful God behind and before. Knowing the intensity of attitudinal and emotional experiences, I shudder to imagine trying to find my way through them via reason (which balks at the first cactus) or by will power (which quails before a looming sandstorm) or by positive thinking (which deflates in the blasting heat).

As we face the wilderness, we who know Jesus Christ as personal Savior have His presence, leadership, and power available to us every moment. How His provision will be needed! There will be daytime stretches of wilderness in which the heat, apart from His cloudy pillar's shade, will drain and defeat us; there also will be night-shrouded times when unknowable dangers, apart from His pillar of fire, will swallow us up. *"Apart from"*—thank God, that phrase never applies. Rather, in daylight or darkness He is *ever near* His children.

The edge of the wilderness, then, while it indicated the *musts* of the journey, also inferred its *marvels.* The great, towering cloud would not just provide shade by day and light by night; it majestically signaled God's presence and leadership moment by moment.

THE

IN VIEW

*They wandered in the wilderness in a solitary way;
they found no city to dwell in.
Hungry and thirsty, their soul fainted in them.
Psalm 107:4-5*

FEAR AT THE RED SEA

As we begin to parallel Israel's pathway, a valid preliminary question arises. Negative emotions and attitudes will mark and mar their different locations along the route. But which is primary—attitude or emotion? I don't believe a clear distinction is possible. Rather, the two blend and interact. The quandary could be said to be reflected in the classic query "Which comes first, the chicken or the egg?" Attitude certainly can gender or strengthen emotion, and emotion just as certainly can give birth to or nurture attitude. In other words, mind and heart are in constant interplay.

Emotions and attitudes are normal functions of our human structure; they are not sinful in and of themselves. Without them, we would be either zombies or robots. Functioning minds create attitude; active internals create emotions. To experience the emotion of fear is not sin. Fear can be a useful emotion—virtually a protective device. Without fear's restraint we would stumble into all sorts of difficulties and dangers. According to the Bible. fear should also be part of genuine worship and faithful obedience.

We will see in Israel's very first encampment, and recognize as present in us, fear that is sinful. Why? Because
we choose both the in-working and the out-working of our
attitudinal and emotional capacity: wherever they defy
God's Word, those *products* of function are sinful.

The marvels of promised divine overseeing can be
quickly forgotten. That was the case when the Israelites
suddenly found themselves experiencing a squeeze play—

> But the Egyptians pursued after them, all the
> horses and chariots of Pharaoh, and his horsemen,
> and his army, and overtook them encamping by the
> sea (Exodus 14:9).

Poor Israel! There they were, barely settled into their
unsettledness, and the thundering of Pharaoh's army
sounded behind them. The chariot wheels rolled forward
with a smooth, confident rumble, because

> Pharaoh will say of the children of Israel, They
> are entangled in the land, the wilderness hath shut
> them in (Exodus 14:3).

How recently have you been there—there in the
wilderness where the Red Sea lies before you and the
enemy's threatening chariot wheels rumble toward you
from behind? Are you in that situation even as you read
this book? Flee with me to His Book.

Israel was camped by the sea. At first the view out over
the shining water must have been refreshingly beautiful—
a welcome change from the desert's expanse. But, in an instant, circumstances changed drastically: Pharaoh's military
powers swept toward them; the sea made escape impossible.
They were caught in a terrifying vise.

That place—that moment of threat—was an awful accident of fate, a horrific happenstance, right? Wrong. *That place* was of God's choosing:

> And the Lord spake unto Moses, saying, Speak
> unto the children of Israel, that they turn and encamp
> before Pi-ha-hiroth, between Migdol and the sea, over
> against Baal-zephon: before it shall ye encamp by the
> sea (Exodus 14:1-2).

God very specifically chose their campsite by the sea.

Any one of us, as well, may suddenly find herself "encamped" in a place of threat. The following could be considered such places:

- Job loss just as major surgery looms

- A husband's death when children range in age from preschool to early teens

- Aged parents moving in to be cared for as children's college costs begin

Whatever it is, that obstacle ahead is awful; the sound of chariot wheels behind is terrifying. But God knows exactly where we are encamped. He is SOVEREIGN—sovereign over the sea, sovereign over the enemy. Yet notice Israel's reactions:

> And when Pharaoh drew nigh, the children of
> Israel lifted up their eyes, and, behold, the Egyptians
> marched after them; and they were sore afraid: and
> the children of Israel cried out unto the Lord. And
> they said unto Moses, Because there were no graves
> in Egypt, hast thou taken us away to die in the wilder-
> ness? wherefore hast thou dealt thus with us, to carry

*us forth out of Egypt? Is not this the word that we did
tell thee in Egypt, saying, Let us alone, that we may
serve the Egyptians? For it had been better for us to
serve the Egyptians, than that we should die in the
wilderness (Exodus 14:10-12).*

The fleeing Israelites grew terribly afraid. They bewailed
the situation in which they found themselves. They were
convinced the circumstances were hopeless. The geography
of attitudes and emotions looks familiar, doesn't it? But
what did this situation *mean* for Israel—and by extension
for us?

First, we can learn a vital lesson about God's people of
yesterday and today: we are weak. When the squeeze
comes, we demonstrate our faithlessness; we experience
panic. All those negatives surface despite the fact that we
claim kinship with the King of kings and the Lord of lords.

Second, we can learn a lesson about God's twofold desire for us in difficult times and places: He wants us to be
quiet and obedient. Moses told the Israelites,

> *Fear ye not, stand still, and see the salvation of
> the Lord (Exodus 14:13).*

Fear can prompt us to rush off blindly in all directions.
Instead, we're to "stand still"—to exert spiritual discipline
and to control the panic reaction. Stillness in viselike situations is neither natural nor easy. The body itself legislates
against it with increased heart rate; quickened, ragged
breathing; trembling legs and hands; sweating; and so forth.
As the mind focuses on the threat, thoughts become a
chaotic jumble. How, then, can you and I be still in threatening situations? By appropriating supernatural infusion:

peace. The Lord Jesus left to His followers the precious gift of peace:

> *Peace I leave with you, my peace I give unto you: not as the world giveth, give I unto you. Let not your heart be troubled, neither let it be afraid (John 14:27).*

Too often, however, we leave the gift beautifully wrapped but unopened in those times when we most need it. Scripture reminds us

> *And let the peace of God rule in your hearts (Colossians 3:15).*

The fear-defying gift of peace is not something given separate from the Giver. Rather, it encircles and fills our heart as we move closer into His great heart's embrace:

> *For he is our peace (Ephesians 2:14).*

As we allow peacefulness to replace fear's many physical manifestations, our mouths are to be still, as well, lest we miss or misunderstand the still, small voice of God.

In each of our Red Sea times, our heavenly Father wants us to reject fear's negatives—not by "commanding the demon of fear," as some would urge, and certainly not by mental contortions to think ourselves out of fear. However broad and deep the sea ahead of us may be, no matter how loudly the army may advance behind us, neither threat determines our fate in the situation. We and the circumstances are in the hand of our almighty, eternal, omnipotent God. He sits unperturbed and unshaken upon His throne.

Following His desire that we in quietness be open to His presence, there is His desire that we be actively obedient despite our state within and without. He says, "Go forward." But let's break the command down into specifics.

- Go forward—not standing fear-frozen into immobility.

- Go forward—not racing in mad rout toward the rear.

- Go forward—not trying to sidle around the difficulty.

Ah, yes, how clearly God says to you and me, "Go forward!" when we're afraid. His admonition against fear is sounded repeatedly throughout the Bible. One of the most powerful and direct challenges is found in Isaiah:

> Fear thou not; *for I am with thee: be not dismayed; for I am thy God: I will strengthen thee; yea, I will help thee; yea, I will uphold thee with the right hand of my righteousness (Isaiah 41:10).*

How many, many times has fear thrown us into frantic, useless motion? How often has it deafened us to what the Bible says? On how many occasions have we panicked and balked at the Red Sea—or a *red puddle*—in our lives?

Fear is not just an academic subject for me: it is, rather, my most plaguing wilderness challenge. Sometimes I laughingly say that it all began when I was born in the breach position. Having originally backed into the world, I have timorously backed through life ever since. Most of life appears Red Sea-like to me, because inborn temperament and childhood scars have coalesced into extreme timidity. Therefore, I treasure the fact that God through-out Scripture so often encourages His people against fear.

Some months ago a ladies retreat attendee passed along a helpful acrostic for timid souls and terrifying times.

F—false
E—evidence
A—appearing
R—real

False evidence of a hopeless situation was all too clear in Israel's sight. There they stood, that great band of newly rescued people. The sound of pursuit was in their ears; the sight of a barrier was in their eyes: they were caught in a vise—the heart-stopping vise of threatened destruction. Such a vise is a tough place, and it demands a hard choice: give way to shrieking, heart-freezing emotion or quietly step forward, exercising the will to obey.

We know that Israel chose correctly: they denied the panic toward which their hearts moved them; they over-ruled the visceral reaction in favor of the spiritual response. That decision was more than just mental decisiveness win-ning out in the struggle. *By faith* they disobeyed the prompt-ings of their human frailty and, instead, obeyed God.

You and I conquer fear in the same way: by turning from the threats around and the thudding heart within, making the mental determination to obey and activating the spiritual discipline to trust. He whom we obey is greater than any enemy, mightier than any obstacle:

> *Wait on the Lord: be of good courage, and he*
> *shall strengthen thine heart: wait, I say, on the Lord*
> *(Psalm 27:14).*

For I the Lord thy God will hold thy right hand,
saying unto thee, Fear not; I will help thee (Isaiah
41:13).

There was marvelous reward for Israel—and there is
for us—in seeing God's victory over the "vise place." The
Red Sea parted, the Israelites safely passed through it, and
the enemy drowned.

On the safe side of the Red Sea, with the Egyptian
threat removed, Israel rejoiced. Moses and Miriam led
them in songs of praise to God. Please take time at this
point to read the words of their songs, found in Exodus
15:1-21.

Moses and the Israelites knew the "vise place" between
pursuing hordes and impassable waters *once*—you and I
may experience it numerous times throughout our lives,
with the names and places changed but the challenge real.
Each recurrence presents the opportunity to look back
upon our first Red Sea time, to take courage from God's
triumph then and there, and to use it to inspire our faith
here and now.

Disappointment at Marah
Ingratitude at Elim

The Waters at Marah

Pharaoh's army and the Red Sea, challenging as they were, barely began the journey: Israel was still only at the *edge* of the wilderness.

The great company of escaped slaves moved on from the Red Sea, hearts high because of God's deliverance from pursuit. For three days they traveled through the wilderness of Shur. The Hebrew word for "Shur" has the basic meaning of "wall." It proved to be a wall of thirst:

> *So Moses brought Israel from the Red sea, and they went out into the wilderness of Shur; and they went three days in the wilderness, and found no water (Exodus 15:22).*

Three days of walking probably covered between thirty and forty miles. Whatever water they carried from their earlier encampment would have been quickly used up or evaporated; thirst became a major factor.

Drying mouths translated into arid spirits: nasty, rotten attitudes. They must have felt immense relief when at last they caught sight of Marah's waters. How eagerly they would have rushed forward, with appointed members of clans and families collecting the precious liquid for their groups. But delight was short-lived: the water was *bitter*. Disappointment over undrinkable water muddied their souls. The people challenged Moses,

What shall we drink? (Exodus 15:24).

You and I experience Marahs, too. Our days of earthly life make us thirsty; we yearn for refreshing. Then, finally, the liquid shine of water is there before our eager eyes. We rush forward and bend to drink—only to find the water worse than the thirst that drove us to it.

Life is filled with places of bitter disappointment. Let's think of just a few representative ones:

- The thirst for a healthy, active life—vs.—the Marah of chronic illness.

- The thirst for sufficient finances—vs.—the Marah of scrape-by living.

- The thirst for marriage—vs.—the Marah of singleness.

- The thirst for wedded bliss—vs.—the Marah of yoked agony.

- The thirst for conception—vs.—the Marah of barrenness.

- The thirst for motherhood—vs.—the Marah of miscarriage or infant death.

- The thirst for godly offspring—vs.—the Marah of rebellious children.

Bitter, bitter is the water of disappointment! And how often we, like Israel, react with muddied spirits.

What is this experience we call "disappointment"? It is an unfulfilled desire, the death of a dream, an exploded expectation, a shattered illusion, a blasted hope, a sensed emptiness we yearn to have filled. All have to do with natural human desires: our perception of need and what we feel necessary to meet that need.

Disappointing circumstances vary greatly, of course, in type and impact. But each one is a wilderness location where we may struggle. Some of our needs are major, genuine, and legitimate. Israel's need for water in the desert was such a need. So are those modern examples listed earlier in this chapter. Other needs are minor—even manufactured and frivolous. Still others rank somewhere between the two extremes. Whatever the nature of the need, we often respond in our thirst to the bitter water of disappointment with grumbling or depression.

Our lips move easily into voicing our disappointments, don't they? However, such a reaction is much more serious than we feel it to be. Inherent in it is the unspoken charge that we have not gotten what we have a right to expect; we have been cheated of something we deserve.

Our *rights*. What we *deserve*. Those words standing alone, pulled out from the qualifying, explanatory phrases in which we typically wrap them, present an unlovely reality. We would each do well to rethink our response to disappointments, whatever they are or have been, and whenever or wherever they occur.

God understands disappointment, just as He understands thirst:

Hope deferred maketh the heart sick (Proverbs 13:12).

Repeatedly, He gives us glimpses into the lives of those who have lived before us; he lets us see into their hearts:

When I looked for good, then evil came unto me: and when I waited for light, there came darkness (Job 30:26).
Lord, why castest thou off my soul? why hidest thou thy face from me? (Psalm 88:14).

God not only understands, however; He *undertakes* for us in our places of disappointment, just as faithfully as He undertook for Israel at Marah. Jehovah pointed the children of Israel to a tree. That tree, thrown into the water, made it sweet.

And he cried unto the Lord; and the Lord shewed him a tree, which when he had cast into the waters, the waters were made sweet (Exodus 15:25a).

If you and I will bring the cross of Jesus Christ to bear upon our waters of Marah, they, too, will be made drinkable. When life's disappointments are bitter, we must turn our tear-filled eyes to the ultimate place of human suffering: the tree of Calvary. See Christ's agony there; see it first as foretold in Isaiah's prophecy, chapter 53: His being rejected, His being wounded for our transgressions, His being bruised for our iniquities. Then go on to the graphic descriptions that God has recorded: Golgotha's agonies as seen by four eyewitnesses—Matthew (27:22-54), Mark (15:9-39), Luke (23:33-47), and John (19:14-30). Rather than simply reading lightly through the accounts, use the

camera of your imagination to go with Jesus. Hear the
rage-filled voices calling for His death; see Him stripped
and beaten bloody; see the purple robe of mockery flung
over His lacerated back; see vicious hands reach out to His
face, ripping great chunks of beard from His cheeks; see
filthy, cursing mouths spit in His face; see the crown of
long, wicked thorns crushed down upon His head, causing
rivulets of blood; see Him dragging the cumbersome, heavy
cross; hear the echoing ring of the hammer as it drives
great spikes through His wrists and feet; finally, watch Him
die there, suspended between the earth and sky, which His
own hands created, so marred as scarcely to appear a
human being. He is looking down through the years at
you, and at me—we for whom He took sin's judgment.

At least two things result when we apply the tree of
Calvary to our disappointments.

First, in contemplating Jesus' sacrificial death, we experience personal reduction: self shrinks from its fleshly
bloat to its spiritual skeleton. Rebuked for a prideful sense
of personal deserving, we are reminded that our only true
deserving is hell—from which the precious blood of Christ
has saved us.

Second, our personal experience is diminished. Even
our most intense suffering cannot be compared to that
which Jesus Christ in love took upon His sinless self. He,
the "man of sorrows, and acquainted with grief" enables us
not only to drink of Marah but also to find it sweet *through
our fellowship with Him in suffering.*

> *Beloved, think it not strange concerning the fiery
> trial which is to try you, as though some strange thing
> happened unto you: but rejoice, inasmuch as ye are*

partakers of Christ's sufferings; that, when his glory shall be revealed, ye may be glad also with exceeding joy (I Peter 4:12-13).

For I reckon that the sufferings of this present time are not worthy to be compared with the glory which shall be revealed in us (Romans 8:18).

As Jesus was "made perfect" through the things He suffered, so shall you and I be molded into His likeness through our sufferings—if we respond with a submissive spirit.

There is probably someone in your sphere of relationships who daily lives out the reality of bitterness made sweet in Christ. I have several precious friends who fit that description. Let me describe them very briefly, without giving their names, in order to let you catch a glimpse of this Scripture principle made vitally personal.

Some years ago, a severely handicapped girl enrolled in Bob Jones University. Although her body was twisted, her mobility made possible only by cart and/or crutches, and her speech slurred, this young woman not only quickly won the heart of everyone on campus; she also became an informal instructor in our midst. With her ready smile, her sweet spirit, and her "God is good!" exclamations, she taught us powerful lessons about God's sufficiency. She made us realize that there is a dimension to living that has nothing to do with the physical and everything to do with the spiritual. Within weeks of her enrollment, she was dubbed "Sunshine." After successfully completing her training, this darling young lady went on to invest her life in full-time ministry to handicapped children.

On one of my first speaking trips to California, I made the acquaintance of a vibrant young preacher's wife. Throughout the retreat she seemed to be everywhere on the site and involved in everything. In watching her and fellowshiping with her, my heart felt a special, warm bonding. When I got home from the retreat, I added her name to my prayer cards. What a shock, shortly thereafter, to learn that she had been stricken with multiple sclerosis. Yet there was not a trace of self-pity, not an iota of shadowed spirit in the letters that continued to come from her. Nor did this dear lady's Marah end with her own ever-worsening condition. Subsequently, her husband and son were in an auto accident that left one a quadriplegic, the other a paraplegic. She who so greatly needed help herself became servant to those she loves. No longer able to write, my precious friend corresponded via cassette tapes, her voice filled with peace and joy.

One of my most prized friendships has been with a pastor's wife who suffered for many years with rheumatoid arthritis. Although an observant eye might notice her swollen knuckles, no one could ever catch a spirit of downheartedness or words of complaint. She never used her pain as an excuse against over-long days of ministry or overly demanding parishioners. In later years her life was further complicated by bouts with cancer herself and in her husband, a parent's and a sibling's death, plus her extensive back surgery. Still, this friend daily shamed me with her soul-deep sweetness, her constant concern for others, and her gratitude for each of God's goodnesses to her.

You can probably think of some who have served similarly to challenge and help you. What a blessed touch such lives have upon ours. They speak eloquently of Calvary's sweetening power for our every Marah.

It was at Marah, after their thirst was quenched, that God addressed the matter of Israel's continuing health.

> *There he made for them a statute and an ordinance, and there he proved them (Exodus 15:25).*

As they had seen the waters of Marah healed by a tree, so they would know their own physical health protected by God if they

- would diligently hearken to His voice,

- would do that which was right in His sight,

- would give ear to His commandments, and

- would keep all His statutes.

As throughout the various aspects of God's covenant relationship with His people, obedience would result in blessing:

> *I will put none of these diseases upon thee, which I have brought upon the Egyptians: for I am the Lord that healeth thee (Exodus 15:26).*

Think about the facets of Jehovah's instructions given here. He presents four requisites: three of them have to do with *hearing and heeding His Word;* only one has to do with *actions.*

Because we largely disregard our spiritual responsibility to read, heed, and obey the Word, God's women today are suffering "Egyptian" diseases of the soul: thoughts as cancerous, spirits as leprous, speech as corrosive, lives as infectious, as those who know not God. We are suffering soul diseases in epidemic proportions, and we don't even have the spiritual sensitivity to know that we're sick!

Our heavenly Father wants us to be *spiritually healthy* children. When our time in, knowledge of, and obedience to God's Word is weak, we are bound to suffer sin's plagues in our soul. In a later chapter, I will give some specific suggestions for fitting Bible reading and study into a busy life.

Whether our Marahs be many or few, major or minor, may the water we drink there be sweetened by the tree of Calvary and our selves strengthened by the Word.

The Oasis at Elim

From the place of tree-sweetened waters, the Israelites moved on to a place where sweet water was abundant.

> And they came to Elim, where there were twelve wells of water, and three-score and ten palm trees: and they encamped there by the waters (Exodus 15:27)

The campsite at Elim, immediately following the one at Marah, not only contrasted sharply in the physical sense; it also commented tellingly upon Israel in the spiritual sense.

The oasis of Elim contained twelve wells and seventy palm trees. God's graciousness is plainly seen in this spot as He provided a rich campsite and pleasant resting place. What an improvement over Marah! God's good provision was unmistakable in His directing them to Elim, where the people enjoyed both abundant water and welcome shade.

But we need to pause, to listen—listen for something we'll not hear. When the Israelites came to such a welcoming, restful place, mightn't they have been moved

to compose poetry or to write songs? Apparently, however, they were silent. There they sat, taking in the blessings but giving out nothing in the way of gratitude or praise.

Ooooops—here we are again, clearly recognizable at Elim! God's tender care is wonderfully demonstrated as He so often grants an Elim following a Marah. At Marah we're full of complaint; at Elim we're empty of praise. Our disappointment over Israel's silence must be tempered by acknowledging God's disappointment over our own, similar silence.

Perhaps my personal confession at this point can serve to illustrate. Following a trouble-free pregnancy and normal birth, our firstborn son failed to survive his struggle to breathe. In spite of the attending physician's valiant efforts, our much-wanted baby died in less than an hour. What a Marah! Within the space of the next six years, however, God graciously gave Elim: three healthy children were born to us. Did the years of Elim's blessings find me always aware of and rejoicing in them? Of course not; they just as often found me fussing about added pressure, lack of time, and so forth. That Elim-like failure has characterized my life time after time.

Because recognition of blessing and gratitude for it seem to be so difficult naturally, I find Scripture helpful not just in its many urgings to praise but also in its providing *words* for my inexpressive tongue. The Book of the Psalms is, of course, full of such passages, and each one I memorize seems sweeter and more appropriate than the one before. One of the passages that has most recently put words in my mouth and gratitude in my heart is Psalm 34.

*I will bless the Lord at all times: his praise shall
continually be in my mouth. My soul shall make her
boast in the Lord.*

*O magnify the Lord with me, and let us exalt his
name together.*

*The angel of the Lord encampeth round about
them that fear him, and delivereth them. O taste and
see that the Lord is good: blessed is the man that
trusteth in him.*

*The eyes of the Lord are upon the righteous, and
his ears are open unto their cry.*

*Many are the afflictions of the righteous: but the
Lord delivereth him out of them all.*

*The Lord redeemeth the soul of his servants: and
none of them that trust in him shall be desolate.*

Marah: a place of bitter water made sweet. May its lesson of applying the tree take deep hold upon our hearts.
Elim: a place of palm trees and water wells. As we pause
there with Israel, may we have eyes ready to recognize our
own many rich oases, and lips ready to rejoice in God's
giving them.

DISSATISFACTION IN SIN

*And they took their journey from Elim, and all
the congregation of the children of Israel came into the
wilderness of Sin, which is between Elim and Sinai,
on the fifteenth day of the second month after their
departing out of the land of Egypt. And the whole
congregation of the children of Israel murmured
against Moses and Aaron in the wilderness: and the
children of Israel said unto them, Would to God we
had died by the hand of the Lord in the land of Egypt,
when we sat by the flesh pots, and when we did eat
bread to the full; for ye have brought us forth into this
wilderness, to kill this whole assembly with hunger
(Exodus 16:1-3).*

Following their brief, palm-filled but praise-empty encampment at Elim, Israel moved on—into the wilderness
of Sin. There they would focus their fussing on their mid-
sections: they would complain of their hunger.

The Hebrew word for "Sin" used here did not have a
moral connotation; rather, it was descriptive of the place—

meaning either "thorny" or "clay." Either description pictures a campsite less than inviting. Too, the new area obviously contrasted with Elim's recent comforts. Thus, the wilderness of Sin must have loomed harshly in Israel's sight. Harsh attitudes soon would be added to harsh surroundings.

In examining the experiences in the wilderness of Sin, we first must consider the factor of time. One and a half months had passed since leaving Egypt. One and a half months—enough time for the wilderness trek to grow tiresome. Enough time for shoulders to ache from lugging belongings through heat and hostile terrain. Enough time for a sense of adventure to wear thin. Enough time to grow weary of daily travel next to some family with obstreperous children, or an individual with an abrasive personality or a nonstop mouth, or . . .

You and I, too, find that time spent in challenging circumstances wears upon us. We think, "If this had lasted for a reasonable period, I could have handled it; but when it drags on. . . ." Let's personalize the wilderness of Sin with some contemporary examples.

- A "quick" kitchen renovation that takes months. The bathroom sink becomes the everything sink; cooking has to be done with a hot plate or Crock-Pot; the refrigerator waits in the garage, where its added power drainage blows the fuses.

- A "temporary" rental or live-with-parents arrangement that stretches into years. A new baby joins the family yearly, putting more demand on space and devastating the savings plans.

- A leaky roof that defies annual fix-it attempts. Finally, exasperation motivates the decision to sell the house. Every prospective buyer, however, comes on a rainy day and sees the leaks, or on a dry day when telltale signs of leakage are still evident.

 A lingering disablement. Endless days and nights of physically demanding care and emotional seesaws.

 A child's "teenage" rebellion that continues into midlife. The prayer request has been made so regularly and so long that fellow church members sigh when it's spoken.

All those many years ago in the wilderness called Sin, with the weight of time adding to their burdens and worsening their walk, Israel plodded forward. To the trudging of their feet was added the grudging of their lips. Let's move in closer so that we can think about God's description:

And the whole congregation of the children of
Israel murmured against Moses and Aaron in the
wilderness (Exodus 16:2).

A million-plus people grumbling! What an awful noise that must have made. But you and I similarly murmur as we walk in wilderness spots of clay or thorns, don't we? Imagine the accumulated complaints from Christians all around the globe as those complaints rise to God's ears!

 Regretfully leaving yesterday's pleasantness

 Resentfully moving forward into today's difficulties

 Glaring around us at the drab landscape

 Feeling irritated by relationship requirements

 Feeling increased animosity toward our leaders

❧ Murmuring, murmuring, murmuring

❧ Worsening the way for ourselves and for others

Much of daily life can resemble desert expanses. We plod along, putting one foot in front of the other mechanically, moving forward by sheer will power—determined to out-grit the sand's grit.

But time is not the only challenging element at this campsite.

In life's monotony and its ceaseless effort, we may grow hungry—not physically, as did Israel, but emotionally. In Israel's case, voice added to voice, until finally there was a unified crescendo of defeatism blurted out to Moses and Aaron:

> And the children of Israel said unto them, Would to God we had died by the hand of the Lord in the land of Egypt, when we sat by the flesh pots, and when we did eat bread to the full; for ye have brought us forth into this wilderness, to kill this whole assembly with hunger (Exodus 16:3).

Does any one of us fail to recognize the people's illogic and extremism expressed here? Of course not; they are obvious. But we fail to see our own similar illogic and extremism. Consider how we may murmur in the packed clay or thorny places of life.

❧ "Boring, boring, boring, that's what it all is! I mean, how many times do I have to wipe this kid's nose? How many times do I have to hear 'Why?' It sure wasn't like this before we started having kids! Ben and I used to be able to *do* things—with each other and with other couples. And my salary made

things a lot easier. Why did I have to give up my
career, anyway? The whole house is looking so . . .
so shabby. Hey, what about taking out a home
improvement loan? I could do it in my own name,
giving references from my single days—and Daddy
would vouch for me."

 "Oh, get off it, Husband Mine! What a change
from the Mr. Romantic role of our courtship days.
Ever since we got married, nothing suits. I'd like to
see *him* handle getting supper on time, just the
right temp, and with nothing but his favorite
meat-and-potatoes bit. Hmmm . . . Anita has been
telling me about those two afternoon soap operas.
She gets so excited over what's happening to the
series characters that she just seems to ignore the
daily grind with her own Mr. Lack-Charm."

"This apartment! It's so sterile. But then, so is my
life—sterile. And the *loneliness!* Married women
really have it made—someone around every
evening, someone to talk to and laugh with.
Hmmm . . . I wonder what James is doing these
days? Sally said he's divorced Alicia—she was a
dip anyway. James and I really had fun together
when we were dating. Maybe I'll see if he's listed
in the telephone directory."

"Type, file, telephone—yuck! I could do all of this
stuff with my eyes shut and my brain in neutral.
I'd give up this crummy job in a minute if there
were something else available. But with rent and
car payments, I can't take time off to look for a
better position. What I'd *really* like is right here,
anyhow. If Diane's position were open, I'd grab
it—and I could do a better job in that office than
she does anyway. I wonder if the boss knows
about Diane's battle with alcohol? She's on the

wagon right now, of course, but with that kind of thing you can never really be sure. I'm going to look in her file—I'll bet she didn't mention her problem on her application. I should let that poor man know what a risk he took in hiring her."

The above situations, given to illustrate our Israel-like illogic and extremism, also expose their inherent danger. Wherever the hunger of dissatisfaction appears in her life, a woman becomes vulnerable to sin: sin first of the spirit and then of the flesh. Are the preceding examples wholly imaginary and thus extreme or invalid? No. Dissatisfaction or discontent may seem only a tiny internal burr when compared to some other negative attitudes—but it is a burr whose bristles can chafe relentlessly and result in major spiritual defection and/or moral failure.

In order to sound a more specific warning, I would remind you how frequently we hear of Christian women who turn to the computer out of boredom. While they may begin simply by seeking something to do, their sense of emptiness makes them vulnerable. The intellectual stimulation and the enjoyment of instant worldwide communication can easily transform into something darker: a chat room connection in which increasingly personal, then intimate, exchanges take place. Her emotional hunger ultimately brings tragedy to her relationship with her husband and to her responsibility toward her children.

Seeing, then, the present seriousness and potential danger of this wilderness encampment, let's examine the various aspects that can mean defeat therein—whether for Israel or for us.

We look back to Egypt and Elim with longing. For those of us saved as adults, there sometimes come backward looks—a yearning for the comparative trouble-free existence of the unsaved years. That is, in "Egypt" we did our own thing, indulging our self-focus to the full, accruing to ourselves whatever emotional, physical, or material benefits we could wangle. As believers, when emotional hunger strikes, we remember Egypt's charms; we forget its chains. Although those of us saved as children have little of Egypt to remember, all of us do experience oases. Any moment in a desert place can tempt us to look back to well-watered spots. In looking back to whatever yesterday, we remember the shade as so cool and refreshing, the water so sweet; today's everything is viewed through the distorting haze of comparative feelings.

We exaggerate benefits in Egypt. The distancing of a few weeks gave Israel a liberally edited memory:

when we sat by the flesh pots

Their phrase indicates abundance; reality had been otherwise. If, indeed, they had ever sat by the flesh pots, the food therein was almost surely being prepared for their masters. As slaves, they would have had few if any opportunities either to sit by or to enjoy the contents of the flesh pots.

We, too, exaggerate "Egypt's" good provisions. Whether we reflect upon our own presalvation yesterday or look around at today's wealthy unsaved world, we magnify those past or imagined benefits and minimize our present blessing. We picture the paths there as carefree—filled with prosperity, play, and possessions; we devalue our own walk's genuine riches—life with eternal significance, peace of heart, treasure in heaven.

We then claim that it would have been better to die in Egypt.

Yet for four hundred years Israel had begged God to free them from Egypt—and they certainly did not mean freedom by death! Did Israel dramatize and exaggerate? Of course. Those are natural byproducts of mental negatives and emotional nuances.

We, too, may heave the inward sigh "I'd have been better off dead rather than go through what I'm experiencing right now." The difficulty against which we react so exaggeratedly may be either great or small: a crippling accident or a blind date's no-show. In fact, we actually may handle a real crisis better than we respond to a minor disappointment.

We accuse our leaders of being deceitful and cruel. "Moses and Aaron, you told us we were escaping Egypt to go to a wonderful place. But you lied! You've brought us out here to the middle of nowhere, and now because we followed you, we're about to die of starvation."

The stretches of everyday life can bring us to similar low points of weariness and craving. For women especially, many places in life can get sand in our shoes and dust in our eyes: our attention to numberless details for self and family; performing mundane, repetitive tasks; the monotony of an unchanging vista. Some days we find the encampment pleasant in its quiet, undemanding familiarity; at other times its very placidity and sameness grow irksome. Our attitude becomes bleak, and our emotions whirl. Then woe to those who lead us! Our leader may be work supervisor, or parent, or husband, or preacher, or mission director. In moments of frustration and discouragement he or she is our Moses, our Aaron. Whatever the name or relationship, that person can become the target for our complaints.

Moses' response to Israel there in the wilderness of Sin cut through any rationalizations they might pose; he addressed the real focus of their attitude. He challenged their core focus:

> Your murmurings are not against us, but against
> the Lord (Exodus 16:8).

The people apparently took little if any note of his words. Do we even today recognize the seriousness of the truth he verbalized? More important, do we *apply* it to our own spirit? Our dissatisfaction—whether voiced or *only* an attitude—really is not against our circumstances or our human leader(s): it is against God Himself—He who towers beyond and above all. What an appalling affront to the God of glory!

The walk we are taking in this book, paralleling Israel's journey and applying its examples to our own lives, is not in any sense a new approach. Long ago, in the very beginning of the Christian era, the apostle Paul wrote instructional letters to believers in various places. He drew freely upon Old Testament history. Writing to the church in Corinth, he warned,

> Neither murmur ye, as some of them also murmured, and were destroyed of the destroyer (I Corinthians 10:10).

Moreover, when Paul wrote to Christians in Philippi, he expanded his urging against dissatisfaction:

> Do all things without murmurings and disputings:
> that ye may be blameless and harmless, the sons of
> God, without rebuke, in the midst of a crooked and

perverse nation among whom ye shine as lights in the world (Philippians 2:14-15).

Expressions of discontent. Murmuring. What an awful sound this must be in the ears of our ever-gracious heavenly Father. In Israel's case God called His people to an accounting for their offense of mind and heart:

> *And Moses spake unto Aaron, Say unto all the congregation of the children of Israel, Come near before the Lord: for He hath heard your murmurings. And it came to pass, as Aaron spake unto the whole congregation of the children of Israel, that they looked toward the wilderness, and, behold, the glory of the Lord appeared in the cloud (Exodus 16:9-10).*

Jehovah in longsuffering spared the people; instead of punishment, He gave them a dramatic, riveting display of His glory. Thus, He reminded Israel that the important thing about the wilderness of Sin was *His presence there.* That was key to the situation: His glorious self should have taken precedence over the setting of clay and thorns. I can look back upon similar experiences, can't you? Not in the sense of a dazzling display in the clouds, of course. But in times and places at which discontentment festered within, I've been brought up short by a powerful reminder of God's all-surpassing greatness. For instance, during a morning of struggle over having to face an especially tough day at the office (my place of clay and thorns), where the desk is piled high with my most-disliked tasks, the Holy Spirit brings to mind Psalm 91:1.

> *He that dwelleth in the secret place of the most High shall abide under the shadow of the Almighty.*

I'm rebuked, quieted, and strengthened: He is with me; His overshadowing presence will enable me to accomplish what's needed throughout the day ahead.

As His majesty shone radiantly in the cloud for Israel, God also demonstrated the magnanimity of His heart:

> And the Lord spake unto Moses, saying, I have heard the murmurings of the children of Israel: speak unto them, saying, At even ye shall eat flesh, and in the morning ye shall be filled with bread; and ye shall know that I am the Lord your God (Exodus 16:11-12).

In response to their dissatisfied hearts and discontented minds, Jehovah promised to provide the things for which they grumbled. Oh, the great, great heart of our loving God!

Difficulties in the wilderness of Sin were real; the people's hunger was a genuine physical need. God didn't change their circumstances; instead, He pointed them to Himself and His ability to provide for them. Though the wilderness would continue to surround them, He was there with them. Though they would continue to need food, He would provide for them. In our personal, private wilderness, even sweeter assurance is extended to you and me:

> For the Lord God is a sun and shield: the Lord will give grace and glory: no good thing will he withhold from them that walk uprightly (Psalm 84:11).

Were we to end our consideration of the wilderness of Sin campsite now, the learning opportunity would be rich indeed. But Scripture holds us there longer, enriching the lessons.

In the evening, following the awe-inspiring cloudy display of God's glory, great flocks of quails appeared and flew into the camp. The people killed them and devoured the meat. Their grumbling tongues temporarily grew still as they tasted of Jehovah's wonderful quail appetizer. The main course was to begin the next morning and continue for all their time in all their places throughout the wilderness. It would consist of a unique, completely nourishing staple: bread. But it would be bread sent directly from God. The special provision was to be received in a special manner:

> Then said the Lord unto Moses, Behold, I will rain bread from heaven for you; and the people shall go out and gather a certain rate every day, that I may prove them, whether they will walk in my law, or no. And it shall come to pass, that on the sixth day they shall prepare that which they bring in; and it shall be twice as much as they gather daily (Exodus 16:4-5).

In following verses we see that God gave Israel a specific procedure for receiving the manna.

- Each person was to gather for himself and for those in his care.

- Everyone was to receive the same daily amount: one omer (about two quarts).

- It was to be gathered in the morning on each of six weekdays.

- It was not to be kept overnight.

- It was not to be gathered on the Sabbath.

Jehovah of course kept His part of the arrangement: His manna supply began the following morning. "Manna" was not the name given by the Provider but by the recipients. God told Israel He would provide bread. (What form did they imagine—loaves?) When on that first morning they beheld the small, seedlike particles on the ground, their response was, "What is it?"—using the Hebrew word "manna."

"What is it?" That surprised questioning finds us there again, right in the middle of Israel. In praying for God's provision of various needs, we often find that the answer is not as we'd anticipated; God in His wisdom often chooses an unexpected form or means of supply. What did we expect—loaves?

Here was God's daily, unfailing food provision for Israel. Here, too, were His specific instructions for receiving it. Surely the people would obey; surely they would gratefully follow the prescribed gathering method. But, alas, no. Some immediately decided their way was preferable to God's way: they gathered enough manna for two days. They may have thought their "simplify-the-project-and-save-energy" choice was sensible. After all, wouldn't it

- reduce the number of manna gatherers jostling one another?

- make the home tent happier on alternate mornings by eliminating the need for early rising?

- enable the family to begin the second day better by not having to wait for food to be gathered?

Reasoning . . . reasoning . . . reasoning—opting for human opinion rather than for humble obedience.

The above "common sense" arguments have a familiar ring. At uncountable places along our life pathway we disregard God's instructions for our life and self. We think up multiple reasons to do things our way. But God watched to see how Israel would obey Him in the matter of small, round bits of food. He likewise watches to see how you and I will obey Him in the details of life. At point after point we choose to disobey.

The most obvious application that comes to mind is in the area of material stewardship. God prescribes that we give at least one tenth of *all* our increase—a tithe—back to Him. That tenth is to be given *first*, "off the top." But how very creative we can be in responding:

- "Ten percent? But if I do that, I won't be able to have a savings account."

- "It makes more sense to wait 'til month's end, so we'll be sure to have enough on hand for any medical emergencies."

- "This bank account interest isn't an increase; I gave some out of each paycheck already."

- "Where does this money really go, anyway? It's supposed to go 'to the Lord,' but it actually supports the pastor."

- "Tithe? That's just a lot of Old Testament legalism."

Reasoning . . . reasoning . . . reasoning—convincing ourselves that our way takes precedence over God's way.

Disobeying and cheating God by defying the tithe principle is only one example of our instruction-adjusting responses to His expressed will.

We don't limit our "creative disobedience" to financial matters. We use it repeatedly and extensively. In essence, we rewrite God's Word. Consider just a few examples.

God's original: Rejoice in the Lord alway (Philippians 4:4).

Our edition: Be fairly pleasant when things go well.

God's original: Be [anxious] for nothing; but in every thing, by prayer and supplication with thanksgiving let your requests be made known unto God (Philippians 4:6).

Our edition: Stay uptight over everything; resort to prayer only in extreme cases.

God's original: And be ye kind one to another, tenderhearted, forgiving one another, even as God for Christ's sake hath forgiven you (Ephesians 4:32).

Our edition: Elbow your way through life, confining compassion to your immediate circle of personal relationships, bearing grudges against any who offend you in whatever way.

God's original: Likewise, ye wives, be in subjection to your own husbands (I Peter 3:1).

Our edition: Give lip service to submission while skillfully manipulating your husband.

Wherever we rewrite God's instructions, we do so with extensive and complicated rationalizing.

In things large and small, the manner in which we go about our daily living either positively demonstrates God's authority over us or denies it. Whether God's leadership is expressed in the form of His direct instructions and prohibitions or is given as more general principles, the rule-and-response interaction is not a rigid form but a living relationship. We are *children* of God and *servants* of the Most High. While there are many specific do's and don'ts, there is one grand underlying principle: in all that we do and in the way we do it, we should be

> *doing the will of God from the heart (Ephesians 6:6).*

Some manna gatherers among the Israelites disobeyed God's will with both heart and hand. In heart they rebelled against Jehovah's instruction. With their hands they gathered manna in the way they chose. But disobedience has a price tag. In Israel's case, it was rotted manna. Maggots and a decaying stench invalidated every rationalization. And for those who chose just a "tiny" disobedience such as waiting until later in the day to do the gathering? They came home empty-handed: ungathered manna melted into nothingness when the desert sun grew hot.

God meant what He said in instructing Israel in the wilderness. Just as certainly, He means what He says in instructing you and me today. How obedient are we? Lest we squirm away from the probing of that query, let's consider another example common to our lives. God says,

> *Speak not evil one of another, brethren (James 4:11).*

But, by complicated mental adjustments we convince ourselves that our whispered expressions of interpersonal irritation, jealousy, competition, and accusation are motivated by innocent observation or even prayerful concern. For example, a woman may say to a fellow church member, "The pastor's wife doesn't ever come to our in-home sales parties. Don't you think she could make it if she really cared much about us? I can tell you one thing for sure—she's not missing the parties in order to do her housework! I dropped in over there the other day, and you wouldn't believe the mess! If a woman can't be a decent housekeeper, how in the world can she be what Pastor needs? Of course, I'm just saying this because I'm so concerned for both of them. We need to pray for her."

As we choose our way rather than God's way at point after point, soul manna—His approval and blessing—evaporates in the scorching heat of our disobedience.

An important part of Jehovah's rules for manna collection and consumption was the Sabbath exception. On the day before the Sabbath, each gatherer was to collect twice as much as usual. The people were to prepare and consume one day's worth, storing the remainder for use on the Sabbath. Unlike the forbidden doubling up on weekdays, that which was gathered and stored for the Sabbath did not rot or have wormy infestation.

The Sabbath was the day of REST, which God built into every week when He created the earth and life upon it. While the people's bodies rested, their inner selves were to focus upon God. It was

a sabbath unto the Lord (Exodus 16:25).

When God provided Sabbath observance, it should have been met with immense gratitude and great rejoicing. After all, the hardness of the way was all too evident, according to the travelers' temper and tongues. Surely, then, this was one commandment that would please them all and be met with happy obedience.

But immediately some of the people disobeyed:

And it came to pass, that there went out some of the people on the seventh day for to gather, and they found none (Exodus 16:27).

The disobedient ones suffered consequences for disregarding God's will. At least three are discernable:

- They went hungry for a full day.
- They turned the day that Jehovah intended for restful celebration into one of restless concern.
- They incurred God's displeasure.

And the Lord said unto Moses, How long refuse ye to keep my commandments and my laws? (Exodus 16:28).

God's plan for a weekly day of rest has remained unchanged throughout all the ages since Creation. We no longer observe the "Sabbath"—the seventh day. That practice ended at Calvary, when Jesus' death perfectly fulfilled the law's demand. Henceforward, the *first* day of the week, His resurrection day, became the day of rest and worship for His followers.

We *are* to honor the Lord's Day—Sunday. Modern Christians generally have become quite casual, if not downright scornful, about a "sabbath unto the Lord." The requirement is shrugged off with a comment such as, "Well, we're under grace, not law." Thus, we who name the name of Christ have no day on which we really obey God's never-canceled command for rest and worship. We change our "rest" day to a catch-up-on-work-or-whatever sort of day. And we change "the Lord's Day" into OUR

day—often even resenting the intrusion of church serv-
ices. The results in our lives parallel those in Israel's.

⚕ We go hungry spiritually. Christianity would be an
immeasurably more powerful force in society if we
as individuals faithfully made one day out of every
seven a time of physical renewal, special feasting
upon God's Word, and personal fellowship with
Him. Our energized bodies, clarified minds, and
deepened spirits could be used by God to "turn the
world upside down" again for Him as in the days of
the apostles.

⚕ We change the Lord's Day into a day of restless
concern. Our tired bodies put strain upon our
overloaded minds. Those minds race back and
forth between the week past and the one to come.
Rather than treasuring the oasis that obedience
offers, we determinedly stay in the sand hills.

⚕ We displease God. That consideration alone
should make us rethink and adjust. With regard to
a weekly day of rest, how would each of us answer
that piercing question posed long ago:

*How long refuse ye to keep my commandments
and my laws (Exodus 16:28)?*

Remember, God asked that question after the first
Sabbath violation there in the wilderness. What must He
be saying these thousands of years later when our disobedience has shrivelled our spiritual roots and pickled our spiritual fruits?

Please know, I am not advocating any specific "standards" of Lord's Day observance. There is already too much
pharisaical rules-making evident in our Christian circles.

But I do believe that if each of us individually would go before the Lord to ask forgiveness for our destructive disregard for His day and humbly seek His desire for our Sundays, our lives would flourish as God-fed and God-led people.

A ministry woman reading this book may protest, "*There's no way* Sunday can be my day of rest! That's necessarily the busiest, fullest day of the week." True. You have been called to serve the Lord with all of your energies on that very day God calls His. The principle He established, nevertheless, holds true: *one* day out of every seven is to be a "sabbath"—a rest day. Ministry people are not exempt. In this, just as in every other area of life, we're to be examples in obedience. Thus, we should make whatever adjustments are necessary to labor only six days a week.

Because my husband and I have struggled in this area in our own ministry life and have also walked beside others in their struggles, my heart burden is great. It's not easy to build a day of rest into full-time ministry. But it is essential. Failing to do so imperils individual well-being, family relationships, as well as ministry effectiveness and longevity.

Many ministry families choose Monday as their "off" day; it answers to the physical and emotional letdown that normally follows Sunday's ministry demands. Others divide their day off into segments: two half-days is a common choice.

Ministry people's rationalizing away God's sabbath requirement is particularly shameful because of our accountability to and example before those we lead. There is also an added dimension of unloveliness in the pride discernable through our rationalizing:

♪ "My position is too important to God for me to take a day off."

♪ "The advancement of God's work depends so much on me that I'm sure He'll understand."

♪ "Ministry excludes me from ordinary obedience requirements."

Scripture reveals that Jesus Christ, who was wholly God and wholly man, not only honored His own body's need for rest and refreshment but also showed His disciples its importance. Consider one interesting incident in Mark 6:31-32. Jesus is speaking to His little group of disciples:

> Come ye yourselves apart into a desert place, and rest a while: for there were many coming and going, and they had no leisure so much as to eat. And they departed into a desert place by ship privately.

A ministry woman can find several important and pertinent things in this passage:

1. It was Jesus Himself who called the disciples aside to rest.

2. They were called from the midst of active ministry (note the description of their busyness).

3. Jesus was inviting them to go apart *with Him* (a key need in our sabbaths, whenever they may be).

4. Their destination was to be a desert place; solitude is implied.

5. Their going aside was just for rest; no seminar, brainstorming, and so forth.

6. Even their mode of transportation was restful because it was private.

Ministry, of course, is to, with, and for people. That
entails specific, unique, and varied pressures. Regular periods of relief from those demands of caregiving are essential.

Neither our circuitous reasoning nor pious-sounding
"explanations" can erase God's statement, that we

> Refuse . . . to keep [His] commandments and
> [His] laws.

In our years of ministry, my husband and I through personal experience and observation of others have been convinced that obedience to the day-of-rest commandment
can transform ministry's effectiveness. It also positively
transforms the *spirit* of ministry. When God's servants
choose to disobey the sabbath principle, we risk physical
burn-out and mental overload; worse, we create within
ourselves shriveled, sour spirits.

The wilderness of Sin—the campsite did not cause
Israel's negative attitude, ungoverned emotion, and disobedience. It simply revealed the clay and thorns within their
hearts. So it is for us. God tells us what to do about that
internal state:

> Sow to yourselves in righteousness, reap in
> mercy; break up your fallow ground: for it is time to
> seek the Lord (Hosea 10:12).

ANGER AND WARFARE AT REPHIDIM

The great throng got on the move again—through and out of the wilderness of Sin. They came next to Rephidim. The problem with that area became immediately apparent:

> And all the congregation of the children of Israel journeyed from the wilderness of Sin, after their journeys, according to the commandment of the Lord, and pitched in Rephidim: and there was no water for the people to drink (Exodus 17:1).

Here was a water problem—again. From the very outset of their journey from Egypt, hadn't God demonstrated His power over water?

- ♫ The water of the Red Sea
- ♫ The water of Marah
- ♫ The abundant water at Elim's oasis

Nevertheless, when the peoples' mouths grew dry again at Rephidim, their *faith* went dry as tinder. And blowing across it came the hot wind of anger:

*Wherefore the people did chide with Moses, and
said, Give us water that we may drink. And Moses
said unto them, Why chide ye with me? wherefore do
ye tempt the Lord? And the people thirsted there for
water; and the people murmured against Moses, and
said, Wherefore is this that thou hast brought us up
out of Egypt, to kill us and our children and our
cattle with thirst? (Exodus 17:2-3).*

"Give us water." You have to wonder just how they
expected the poor man to do that! However, rather than
focus upon the controversy at this point, let's instead consider what was happening within the group itself.

Apparently, from what Moses said to God, "they be
almost ready to stone me," the people had moved beyond
the displeasure they had displayed in Sin's wilderness. The
move was a deadly one: advancement into full-fledged
anger.

You and I recognize the ugliness of anger when it is
blatant and boisterous, as it was in the case of Israel: anger
that flares suddenly and expresses itself in snarling or
shouting, in a flushed face, flashing eyes, and rigid body.
We realize that such emotional volatility should not char-
acterize a genuinely born-again woman. We agree that

*an angry man stirreth up strife, and a furious
man aboundeth in transgression (Proverbs 29:22).*

However, our avoidance of or control over fury's ex-
plosiveness may be merely a surface thing.

In Christian circles, we determinedly squash the shameful flame of raw anger, sublimate it, reform it by force of
will, and allow it to see the light of day only in some ac-

ceptable disguise. We dress it up, calling it "hurt," or "disappointment," or . . . But wherever anger's coals lie banked, there will be destructive results. Sooner or later there will come a Rephidim; long restrained anger will have its way—and its say—as it did in Israel's attack upon Moses. There will be subtler, more widespread effects as well.

We often harbor angry feelings as a way to "get back at" unpleasant people or circumstances. However, our anger alleviates neither; instead, it complicates and worsens everything. Too, our abiding irritation negatively influences those around us who aren't even remotely connected with the situation.

I believe that covert anger plays a major, growth-blocking role in many Christian women's lives. It hides behind sweetly smiling faces, spiritual terminology, and nonstop church involvement. But oh, the dark trail of destruction it leaves! Let's consider some real-life examples:

> Paula loudly and endlessly berates anything that doesn't fit her personal concept of holiness. She is quick to condemn Mrs. C. for wearing slacks while gardening, and Miss W., whose earrings are over-large, and Mrs. T., who dresses her two-year-old daughter in above-the-knee outfits, and Miss S., whose lipstick is too shiny, and . . . But behind her purported concern for holiness is anger: resentment harbored for her own girlhood under oppressive parents.

> Anita daily assails her three daughters, warning against friendship with boys; she brings to their attention every newspaper or TV item involving men's mistreatment of, neglect of, or attacks upon women; she badgers them to tell her of any untoward attention paid them by male persons of

whatever age. Her over-protective, fear-producing spirit is fed by anger: in her teens a boyfriend jilted her, and she struggles in a difficult marriage.

🎵 Martha smiles bravely to fellow pastors' wives during their get-togethers, reporting discouraging-but-not-defeating difficulties in the church ever since the assistant pastor and his family were called to a different ministry. She alludes to her expanded responsibilities in taking up the slack and requests prayer for numerous church members "poisoned" by the departed family. Beneath the martyred surface lies intense anger: seething resentment over the failed ministry partnership and personal friendship.

🎵 Letitia battles recurring bouts with depression, despite the fact that she has a circle of supportive friends, a good Bible-preaching church with a strong singles program, and a responsible job in a large office, where she consistently receives merit promotions. In public she admits to minor "downs," intimating a genetic cause. Her roller-coaster emotional mechanism, however, actually runs on the rails of anger over her lifelong singleness.

These examples illustrate only a few of the many ways women may harbor disguised anger—either intentionally or unintentionally. God's Word itself indicates that anger adopts many forms and appears in varying types and degrees:

> Let all bitterness, and wrath, and anger, and clamour, and evil speaking, be put away from you, with all malice (Ephesians 4:31).

Read through the descriptive words again: *bitterness* (marked by resentment or cynicism), *wrath* (forceful, often vindictive anger), *anger* (a strong feeling of displeasure or hostility), *clamor* (a vehement expression of discontent or protest), *evil speaking* (spiteful gossip), *malice* (a desire to harm others or to see others suffer). God warns the Christian against anger's many personalities. Obviously, this is not a simple emotion; one or more of its facets can easily translate into a *spirit* of anger. The passage makes clear that we must not harbor such a spirit.

It is impossible to read Scripture without finding that the God of love is also the God of wrath. His wrath, however, is not the fickle, petulant emotionalism we know; it is a righteous expression of His burning holiness:

> God is angry with the wicked every day (Psalm 7:11b).

Experiencing the emotion of anger is unavoidable: it is a natural element in our human composition. But Scripture exhorts Christians to maintain certain boundaries with regard to anger.

First, there is the boundary of controlled expression and limited time:

> Be ye angry, and sin not: let not the sun go down upon your wrath: neither give place to the devil (Ephesians 4:26).

If you and I would obey just this one prescriptive verse, we would spare other people the pain of our angry words and harsh actions. We would also spare ourselves countless hours of internal turmoil and the complicated consequences of that turmoil.

Second is the boundary of deliberation:

> He that is soon angry dealeth foolishly (Proverbs 14:17).
> He that is slow to wrath is of great understanding: but he that is hasty of spirit exalteth folly (Proverbs 14:29).

Probably neither you nor I need look far to see that truth personally illustrated. For instance, if a driver cuts us off in traffic, we might angrily honk the horn, gun the engine, race past the offender, and make a scowling face as we pass.

> He that is slow to anger is better than the mighty; and he that ruleth his spirit than he that taketh a city (Proverbs 16:32).

How clearly God assures us of our internals' importance. He who constantly monitors the heart applauds our successful struggles therein.

> A wrathful man stirreth up strife: but he that is slow to anger appeaseth strife (Proverbs 15:18).

Internal anger delights to export itself. One wrathful person, either subtly or blatantly, can stir those around her to emotional warfare.

> Be not hasty in thy spirit to be angry: for anger resteth in the bosom of fools (Ecclesiastes 7:9).

In our human frame, testiness comes very easily to us, and we demonstrate foolish pettiness in hair-trigger, angry responses.

Third is the boundary of example and influence:

*Make no friendship with an angry man; and with a
furious man thou shalt not go: lest thou learn his ways,
and get a snare to thy soul (Proverbs 22:24-25).*

Harbored anger is like a deadly virus; it has the power to
infect all who come within its reach. We're warned to recognize its presence and avoid its contamination. In its negative aspects, anger is indeed "just one letter from danger."

We can see something more in Israel's anger at
Rephidim: the emotion's tendency to distort reality, to
shift blame.

Our human ire, sparked by whatever small or large
occurrence, often flicks out to blame others while casting
ourselves as victims. The thought process goes something
like this: it's not *our* fault we're in this mess . . . We were
only doing what we were told to do . . . The whole thing
made perfectly good sense, and if that other person hadn't
. . . Since the whole thing is her (or his) fault, she (or he)
must solve the problem—now! Our angry accusations and
insistences grow worse each time we think about our
predicament—until our spirit becomes so enflamed that
the person we blame might echo Moses' words to the Lord,

they be almost ready to stone me.

Is this an extreme comparison? Not really. We may not
voice our accusations; we may instead stifle anger's flame
to an ever-present, internal slow burn of resentment, dis-
like, or antagonism. Or we may tone down the blame-shift
with double talk. For example, "I've searched my heart, but
I really feel that I acted in all sincerity; of course I never
dreamed that she would do what she did." But God isn't

fooled; He focuses upon our attitudes and emotions in the Rephidims of life. He sees our harbored anger and hears our blame-shifting excuses. Both displease Him, just as Israel's did.

It is convicting to see that while the children of Israel demonstrated fury at Rephidim, Jehovah demonstrated faithfulness. He told Moses to take the elders and go to the rock called Horeb. With the same divinely empowered rod he had held out over the Red Sea for its parting, Moses was to strike the rock. He followed God's instruction, and water gushed forth in abundance. How great is God's forbearance with His unlovely people! One of the history psalms gives insight into His great heart:

> He opened the rock, and the waters gushed out; they ran in the dry places like a river. For he remembered his holy promise, and Abraham his servant (Psalm 105:41-42).

While we fuss and fume over our "Rephidim" difficulties, God is ever faithful, ever true to His promises, ever abundant in His provision for us.

The Israelites' murmuring lips temporarily stilled as they drank the water God provided. Then, suddenly, their life in the wilderness became much more than either food or drink. As if from nowhere, Amalek's nomadic tribe attacked the encampment. War threatened in the wilderness!

Often the enemy's sudden attack comes in our Rephidims too. That is, while partaking of God's most recent provision, all at once quietness turns into pitched battle. Some illustrations may help personalize the Amalek experience.

2. In answer to prayer, Stephanie's barrenness has ended, and she gives birth to her first child. She barely gets the baby home to its carefully prepared nursery, however, before she begins to reel under a multipronged invasion: the baby has severe, chronic colic, destroying peace by day and sleep by night. Her husband Ted's exhaustion makes him irritable, and her maternal focus arouses his jealousy; he becomes petulant and demanding. Her mother-in-law calls long distance every day; she asks questions and makes comments about the baby's continual loud fussiness, inferring that her daughter-in-law lacks maternal skills. The sudden increase in household expenses stresses the budget. Stephanie feels drained physically and emotionally. Her nerves are strained to the breaking point.

2. Following a relaxed, fun-filled family vacation, Marianne hasn't even unpacked the suitcases before the barrage begins: the houseplants, despite promised care by a neighbor, droop lifelessly. The laundry room is flooded with two inches of water due to a burst washing machine hose. Johnny runs in the back door yelling that Mr. Nelson, their vacation dog-sitter, had to take Bruno to the vet twice for treatment after the dog somehow ingested poison. Teenager Esther comes out of her bedroom crying after talking on the phone to her best friend; their family is being transferred to the East Coast. A trail of large black ants marches along the edge of the kitchen floor, up the wall, around the sink, and into the food cabinet. Marianne feels as if an eighteen-wheeler has rolled over her and crushed all the joy and relaxation of their vacation days.

2. The church ladies' retreat has been a real spiritual
mountaintop for Jennifer. In the opening session
she repented of sinful allowances that had crept
into her life, and she committed herself to a closer
walk with the Lord and more godly living as wife
and mother. But when she arrives home, cars and
motorcycles fill the driveway and spill out onto
both sides of the street. A teenage pizza party is
taking place in the house: teens, food, and soft
drinks are in every room except the study, where
her husband Joe sits watching a ballgame on his
TV. Squeals from the backyard signal that the three
younger children are having a party of their own: a
garden hose and water gun battle involving seven
children and four dogs—all of whom are soaking
wet. The telephone rings; it's the secretary of the
junior high school asking if Jennifer can substitute
for a sick teacher next week. A wave of dismay
sweeps over her; tears fill her eyes as her resolve
against angry outbursts threatens to slip away.

Do any of those scenarios parallel your experience?
Such times and places represent our Rephidims and the
attack of Amalek.

Israel's response to Amalek's threat was twofold: some
went out to fight the attackers; others maintained appeal
to God. Both responses were needed then and are needed
now. The Amalekites were descendents of Esau—an ag-
gressive nomadic people well versed in desert warfare.
When unopposed, they overran and conquered their chosen victims: so the nonaggressive Israelites, under Joshua's
leadership, were forced to do battle. Meanwhile Moses,
Aaron, and Hur mounted a hill that overlooked the battleground. There, Moses held up his hands, one containing
the rod of God-empowered leadership, toward heaven. As

long as his hands were aloft, Israel was victorious; when his hands lowered, the tide of battle turned and Amalek gained the advantage. As the warfare continued, Moses' weary arms began to fall. Aaron and Hur stepped in to provide practical assistance: they positioned a stone to serve as a seat for Moses, and then they stood on either side of him and held up his hands.

When Satan comes against our soul with his hordes, our response should wisely parallel Israel's battle at Rephidim. We need to undertake both counteroffensives. First, we must behave as true soldiers of Christ and face the enemy's onslaught, not flee or hide:

> Submit yourselves therefore to God. Resist the
> devil, and he will flee from you (James 4:7).

Simultaneously, we must earnestly and consistently petition the Lord's help. It may be, too, that we need to enlist helpers in our prayer efforts. The apostle Paul, that towering servant of God, did not hesitate to request assistance in prayer:

> Finally, brethren, pray for us, that the word of
> the Lord may have free course, and be glorified, even
> as it is with you: and that we may be delivered from
> unreasonable and wicked men: for all men have not
> faith (II Thessalonians 3:1-2).

How blessed it is to have one or more prayer partners at times of special need! In fierce, private hours of battle you don't even need to be specific when turning to such helpers—but simply call "Help! I need you to pray for me."

Our warfare at "Rephidim" may get hot, long, and heavy, but we will ultimately know victory if we faithfully battle both practically and prayerfully.

Is there more we can learn from Israel's Rephidim? Yes—a further personal message. After victory over the Amalekites, when the encampment again grew quiet, God told Moses to record the victory:

> Write this for a memorial in a book, and rehearse it in the ears of Joshua (Exodus 17:14).

"Write this for a memorial in a book." Several times already we have noted how quickly human beings forget. The fog of forgetfulness rolls in to hide even the most glorious of God's blessings. Here, then, is His own suggested antidote for a poor memory: written records. We are not told how often the written account of victory at Rephidim was used to encourage and bless Israel in general and Joshua in particular through the years that followed. But the record has reached far beyond that immediate time. It has reached down the corridors of centuries and into the room of the present, refreshing our hearts.

"Write this for a memorial in a book." Each of us can profit spiritually by keeping a written record of God's working in our life. We can be motivated for such a project by recognizing

- our tendency to forget specifics of God's dealings,

- the certainty that difficulties will face us in the future, and

- today's personal experiences can infuse courage, patience, and strength for tomorrow.

A spiritual journal can also add a strategic dimension to personal devotions. Daily private time spent with the Lord primarily consists of listening to Him (by studying the Word) and talking to Him (by praying). A daily written record *memorializes the meeting between one's soul and God.*

What, exactly, is such a journal? It is neither fancy nor formal, lengthy nor artistic; rather, it is simply putting your heart's intake on paper. Each day as we get alone with God to seek His instruction and help for life, one or two precepts will stand out as being particularly meaningful. Write them down: the Bible reference, the specific personal application, the spiritual need met or lesson learned, your expression of gratitude. That's it—no big investment, nothing to be seen by anyone else—yet such a recording of daily nuggets becomes a spiritual gold mine.

Israel's written account of Rephidim recorded their one specific victory in battle. The memorial would also provide a twofold brightening in their look to the future. That is, it would not only point them toward their own future victorious engagements with the Amalekites but also to that time when God would fulfill His statement's end:

> For I will utterly put out the remembrance of
> Amalek from under heaven (Exodus 17:14).

A personal spiritual journal does the same. Each time we reread an account from its pages we're blessed by recalling the specific experience and bolstered for future encounters with the enemy. Furthermore, we gain the *eternal* perspective: our plaguing spiritual Amalek will one day be vanquished, finally and totally!

In addition to a written memorial, Moses built an altar, a place of worship. He called the altar Jehovah-nissi—"The Lord Our Banner."

In calling God "The Lord Our Banner," Moses simultaneously offered praise for their first victory over Amalek and claimed the name of Jehovah as Israel's military insignia. He thus indicated active faith for future battles.

When God brings me through a spiritual battle, I should genuinely *worship Him* for the victory given, recognizing and rejoicing in the fact that supremacy over Amalek is *His,* not mine. I should take each post-battle opportunity to raise God's standard as a testimony to His faithfulness. And, under His banner, I will find strengthened faith to move forward, confident *in Him.*

LAW AND IDOLATRY AT SINAI

In the third month, when the children of Israel
were gone forth out of the land of Egypt, the same day
came they into the wilderness of Sinai. For they were
departed from Rephidim, and were come to the desert
of Sinai, and had pitched in the wilderness, and there
Israel camped before the mount (Exodus 19:1-2).

Israel's encampment in Sinai's wilderness would produce
sweeping drama. Its individual scenes hold wall-to-wall (or
cactus-to-cactus) lessons for us as we watch the drama un-
fold. This is the place where God met with Moses on the
mountaintop. There with His own hand He wrote the Ten
Commandments on stone tablets. There Aaron allowed the
people to build a calf of gold and to engage in its idolatrous
worship. There God sent sweeping destruction to punish
His disobedient people.

While modern Christians tend to minimize Sinai, such
an attitude drains the Christian faith of meaning and
power. Ours is a Judeo-Christian heritage. God's dealings
with and instructions to Israel in the Old Testament are
foundational to genuine Christianity.

Sinai's law identifies sin and shows that man is helpless to cleanse himself; God's righteous judgment demands
punishment by death; it can be averted only by the death
of a substitute. Innocent blood shed for sin's forgiveness
builds the bridge between the Old Testament and the New
Testament. In the Old Testament, animals or birds fulfilled
the demand. In the New Testament, God's Son, Jesus
Christ, fulfilled the law's demands by His sinless earthly
life and saves a repentant, believing individual by His sacrificial death on Calvary.

Ignoring or discounting Sinai weakens our Christian
faith in several ways:

- by allowing us a frivolous, faulty concept of God.

- by letting us downplay His hatred for sin.

- by obscuring the severity of His chastisements.

- by minimizing our obligation to obey Him.

Exodus 19:4 calls Israel to remember what they have
seen of God's care to this point. Jehovah describes, through
Moses, what He has done in the days since they left Egypt:

> And how I bare you on eagles' wings, and
> brought you unto myself.

I bore you on eagles' wings. It's interesting how Jehovah
here describes the people's journey. Judging by their attitudes and actions, the Israelites themselves would have
described things far differently: they would have spoken in
terms of forbidding landscape, laborious burden bearing,
parching thirst, gnawing hunger. But God declares them to
have been borne on eagles' wings.

Have you and I sensed eagles' wings under us in traversing our emotional wilderness? Probably no more than Israel did in their geographical wilderness. But *the wings are there.* The lack is not of wings beneath us but of wisdom within us. Israel could have sensed Jehovah's wings if they had focused on Him rather than on themselves and their surroundings. The same is true of you and me in our life journey. Such wisdom-directed focus will enable us to experience the blessed reality of Isaiah 40:31—

> *But they that wait upon the Lord shall renew*
> *their strength; they shall mount up with wings as*
> *eagles; they shall run, and not be weary; and they*
> *shall walk, and not faint.*

It would be fitting for us now—however belatedly—to render praise to Him whose strong, sure wings have lifted and borne us through all.

And how I bare you on eagles' wings.

What a beautiful word picture! How I yearn to have the kind of sensitive heart that senses God's eagles' wings moment by moment *within* my every wilderness.

Look closely now at the second phrase God used in speaking to Israel of their wilderness pathway:

And brought you unto myself.

That statement must have startled the dust-filled eyes and gravel-gritted hearts of the travelers! Every one of Israel's wilderness experiences revealed a core contrast: their insufficiency versus Jehovah's all-sufficiency. The struggles, the threats, the yearnings—all gave them the opportunity to recognize their need of Him and to be drawn to Him. God wants to do the same in our wilderness of attitudes and emotions. Every wilderness spot can be a blessed opportunity to learn of our littleness and His greatness. Again, we are reminded that God's perspective is unlike ours. He makes that declaration when He says,

> For my thoughts are not your thoughts, neither are your ways my ways, saith the Lord. For as the heavens are higher than the earth, so are my ways higher than your ways, and my thoughts than your thoughts (Isaiah 55:8-9).

Our humanity makes us perceive wilderness as terrain that is empty—empty even of God. Jehovah's words about His sustaining reveal just the opposite to be true: however strongly we may sense the vastness of our wilderness, and however alone we may feel there, in a real sense that place is both intimate and full because of our loving Lord's own presence.

Why should we so persistently focus upon the brambles, sand, and heat of our internal landscape? It was in that very landscape we met the Lord Jesus and accepted Him as personal Savior. Yes, our body may have moved down a church aisle, or knelt beside our bed—but the real transaction was one *within the soul:* the eternal Father applied the cleansing blood of His Son and gave the Holy Spirit to dwell within us. Thus, no matter how sharp the brambles, how deep the sand, or how intense the heat at any particular "encampment," it is *there*—within—that we also experience His drawing us near to Himself.

After reminding Israel of His marvelous purpose and His faithful undertaking for them, God proceeded to enunciate the covenant relationship He desired between Himself and His people. His part of the covenant was to make Israel His "peculiar treasure." Their part was obedience.

> *Now therefore, if ye will obey my voice indeed,*
> *and keep my covenant, then ye shall be a peculiar*
> *treasure unto me above all people: for all the earth is*
> *mine (Exodus 19:5).*

Jehovah's transaction at Sinai was the covenant of law. His transaction at Calvary was the covenant of love. We come into personal covenant relations with God on His terms. A covenant is essentially an agreement between two parties. The new covenant demands that an individual agree with God on several points: she is a sinner, hopeless and helpless. She recognizes Jesus Christ as her only means of salvation. She seeks God's pardon for her sin through Jesus Christ, her sin substitute. The Holy Spirit, the third person of the Trinity, affixes the "signature" to the covenant, and He takes up residence in the believer. God through the apostle Peter describes our new covenant identity:

> *But ye are a chosen generation, a royal priest-*
> *hood, an holy nation, a peculiar people; that ye should*
> *show forth the praises of him who hath called you out*
> *of darkness into his marvelous light (I Peter 2:9).*

In order to show forth Christ's praises and to demonstrate that we are indeed His "peculiar treasure," we *as individual believers must obey God's commands as presented in His Word.*

> *But whoso keepeth his word, in him verily is the*
> *love of God perfected: hereby know we that we are in*
> *him (I John 2:5).*

The indwelling Holy Spirit gives us the desire and the ability to obey. Without personal obedience to Scripture, we are not the Lord's treasure at all—we're just peculiar.

Exodus 19:8 records Israel's response to Jehovah's covenant conditions:

All that the Lord hath spoken we will do.

Agreement to obey came quickly, and no doubt it was sincere. After being without identity or sense of worth for four hundred years of slavery in Egypt, Israel was eager to "be somebody special." In focusing on that wonderful opportunity, they gave scant thought to the real meaning of their pledge.

Our human frame, too, leans strongly toward the wonderful *privileges and promises* of God in our relationship with Him, but away from the everyday *practices* of godliness. Our expectation tends to be toward instant, effortless health, wealth, and wisdom. When experience proves to be otherwise, we may rebel. So it proved to be with Israel.

Basking in their avowed faithfulness, the children of Israel briefly became happy campers there at the foot of Mount Sinai. Then God called Moses to the top of the mountain again for two sets of instructions: one for building God-pleasing human beings, the other for building the God-indwelt tabernacle.

Jehovah presented a blueprint for any individual seeking to please Him and experience His blessing. It was given in the form of the Ten Commandments. God's own hand inscribed them upon tablets of stone.

*And he gave unto Moses, when he had made an
end of communing with him upon mount Sinai, two*

tables of testimony, tables of stone, written with the
finger of God (Exodus 31:18).

The cloud-shrouded mountaintop, however, contrasted
sharply with what was happening at its sunny base. At the
base of the mountain all was not well. Sinai's geographical
altitudes at summit and base were very different; so were
the spiritual altitudes. Moses' mind and heart met with
God in indescribable exaltation; the people's minds and
hearts were earthbound to the point of degradation.

Moses' forty days' absence chafed the Israelites. Picture
it. For the first time, their leader had left them; they were
on their own. Although they had fussed at him earlier, his
absence was disturbing. The days dragged on; this encampment was becoming uncharacteristically long. They grew
restless. Although they questioned within themselves and
with others, there seemed no compelling reason for the
lengthy stay there or for Moses' lengthy absence. They
grew resentful. Their restless, resentful attitude ignited
rampaging emotion. From the human standpoint, we can
imagine several contributing factors:

- frustrated curiosity
  ("What's going on up in that cloud, anyway?")

- impatience
  ("A leader's supposed to be *with* us.")
  ("I'm tired of this place!")

- boredom
  ("Here we sit—chores done, talked out.")

Finally, while Moses communed aloft with the living
God, the people constructed an earthen god and wor-
shiped it.

Israel's choice of a calf as idol reflected pagan practices of the day. Not only in Egypt but also in many other contemporary civilizations, the form of a young bull symbolized vitality and strength *through physical fertility*. In modern terms, it was a sex symbol. Their worship reflected the idol's character: it was a sexual orgy.

What about our own "bull calves"? Although we consider ourselves worshipers of God, in actuality we all too easily transfer our allegiance to idols. Certainly, we're horrified at thoughts of a clay, stone, or metal god; our idolatry is much subtler. We worship our desires; we live in pursuit of that which pleases us instead of that which pleases God. We worship our opinion; "I think" or "I don't see why" takes precedence over *"Verily, I say unto you."* We worship our husbands; we practice a false form of "submission," supporting his unbiblical spirit and demands. We worship our home; we pour our time, effort, and money into its maintenance or its expansion, neglecting God's work stateside and abroad. We worship our children; we allow them to do and to have whatever they want, disregarding God's instructions for discipline. We defy outside authority, protecting our kids from consequences of their behavior. We worship our profession; we focus mind and heart upon advancement, recognition, or salary. We worship our denomination; we identify ourselves by denominational name rather than by Christ's name. We worship our church; we maintain our membership in and support of our church despite unbiblical preaching or ungodly music. We worship our preacher; we remain loyal to the man though he becomes disloyal to God in word or act. We worship our "standards"; we scorn those who don't see things exactly as we do. We set ourselves up as judges of their spirituality.

In the eyes of the great I AM, any and all such worship is as horrid and offensive as bowing before the golden calf! God declares repeatedly in His Word that *He will not share His glory with anyone or anything.*

> *I am the Lord: that is my name: and my glory will I not give to another, neither my praise to graven images* (Isaiah 42:8).

Moses at last came down from the mountaintop. His eyes, which had seen unspeakable wonders, suddenly saw unspeakable horrors. His shock must have been truly awful as he descended from Jehovah's glory to Israel's ghastliness. The stone tablets he carried crashed to the ground. Their shattering surely echoed the shattering of his heart.

Wherever we are in our spiritual life or in spiritual leadership, Israel at Sinai should serve as a warning: we are personally vulnerable. Negative attitudes and fluctuating emotions constantly threaten our spiritual strength. Moreover, Aaron's participation in the people's idolatry reminds us that *any human leader,* while claiming to serve God, actually may be fashioning a false god and encouraging our idolatry. Sadly, current days provide numerous examples of such failed leadership. God-blessed ministries can degenerate into personality cults in which the leader's name is spoken and extolled more than God's. A leader can gradually transform a ministry into preacher-king extremism in which he demands absolute loyalty and strict obedience to his proclamations. Or a ministry can so concentrate upon selected areas and so emphasize certain concepts that it becomes unbalanced and deteriorates into "issues" worship.

God's anger raged against idolatrous Israel; He threatened to extinguish them from the earth and establish an entirely new people through Moses. Although Moses' fervent intercessory prayer spared them from total devastation, Jehovah nevertheless punished His erring people. The price of their idolatry was high: three thousand men were killed, and many more suffered from a continuing plague.

> And the Lord plagued the people, because they made the calf, which Aaron made (Exodus 32:35).

In our personal idolatry we do not experience the sword or the plague—but we do pay. Christianity as a whole suffers; each individual influences the entire body of Christ; weakness or failure in that one becomes weakness in the whole. Christianity's paling testimony around the world is undeniable; it is being outpaced in many places by false religions. Churches and other local ministries stagger and limp. Families turn upon themselves and cannibalize their own: God-forgetful adults make their marriage a battleground; they break the marriage bond; they discourage their children's spiritual growth through indifference or opposition. Individuals endure the agonies of contorted relationships and scavenged existence: one marriage partner suffers constant pressure and indignities from the Scripture-defying spouse; a personable "king pin" leader coerces subordinate ministry personnel into questionable financial or ethical practices. All those and more are the price we're paying for tolerating false gods.

There at the foot of Mount Sinai Israel presented a three-dimensional, full-color picture of sin's grip upon mankind and the need for a clear, simple (not *easy*, but simple) guideline for living. Before it could even be enunciated publicly, the guideline lay on the ground, broken in pieces.

Yet again, however, the mighty Creator God stooped to the littleness of His creatures; He graciously rechiseled the tablets of the law.

The Ten Commandments

How unique is God's law! Even strictly in the structural sense, it proclaims its authorship. In just ten succinct instructions Jehovah set forth His unchanging standard for all time: the measurement for divine acceptance. The human tendency toward verbiage would have demanded a whole mountainside of stone for the inscription! How, after all, could mortal mind even hope to express what God traced in stone that day: *perfection in the sight of the Lord.* You and I need to look seriously, personally, and contemplatively at the commandments (Exodus 20:2-17). We need to consider how each one applies specifically to the area of our greatest spiritual challenge: our wilderness of emotions and attitudes.

First

> *Thou shalt have no other gods before me.*

Second

> *Thou shalt not make unto thee any graven image, or any likeness of any thing that is in heaven above, or that is in the earth beneath, or that is in the water under the earth: thou shalt not bow down thyself to them, nor serve them: for I the Lord thy God am a jealous God, visiting the iniquity of the fathers upon the children unto the third and fourth generation of them that hate me; and showing mercy unto thousands of them that love me, and keep my commandments.*

If we consistently obeyed just the first two command-ments, our wilderness threats would be greatly reduced. No matter the particular "encampment" experience, we could know both personal triumph and positive testimony. Our every failure begins at this point, just as Israel's did: we choose to look away from Jehovah, the one true God, to the ever-alluring god of self. That fickle, demanding deity delights in rampant emotions and corrosive attitudes.

Third

> *Thou shalt not take the name of the Lord thy*
> *God in vain; for the Lord will not hold him guiltless*
> *that taketh his name in vain.*

While we abhor the thought of verbal cursing, we may unwittingly blaspheme God's holy name by our attitudes or our emotion-motivated actions. The Lord makes that clear in a passage specifically addressed to women:

> *The aged women likewise, that they be in behav-*
> *iour as becometh holiness, not false accusers, not*
> *given to much wine, teachers of good things; that they*
> *may teach the young women to be sober, to love their*
> *husbands, to love their children, to be discreet, chaste,*
> *keepers at home, good, obedient to their own hus-*
> *bands,* that the word of God be not blasphemed
> *(Titus 2:3-5).*

What a riveting exhortation! We must constantly be aware that the individual Christian's life speaks either a blessing or a curse upon God's name.

Fourth

> *Remember the sabbath day, to keep it holy. Six days shalt thou labour, and do all thy work: but the seventh day is the sabbath of the Lord thy God: in it thou shalt not do any work, thou, nor thy son, nor thy daughter, thy manservant, nor thy maidservant, nor thy cattle, nor thy stranger that is within thy gates: for in six days the Lord made heaven and earth, the sea, and all that in them is, and rested the seventh day: wherefore the Lord blessed the sabbath day, and hallowed it.*

God here expands upon the statute He presented earlier. Faithful obedience to the one-day-of-rest requirement has a profound, positive effect upon our internals as well as upon our physical well-being.

Fifth

> *Honour thy father and thy mother: that thy days may be long upon the land which the Lord thy God giveth thee.*

To this point, the commandments focus upon our relationship to God. Now they take up our relationship with other people. The first consideration addresses the parent-child connection. Note that there is no time limitation indicated; honor for parents is to be lifelong. Probably the greatest challenges in the sense of attitudes and emotions to our obeying this command are in three areas. First, parental failures: whether it was abuse, neglect, abandonment, favoritism, or some other failure, a child's mind and heart struggle to maintain honor for the offending parent.

Second, our teen years are not only tough in handling emotions and attitudes generally; they're also often marked by difficulties in honoring parents. Pre-adult years find us thinking that our parents are prehistoric in their expectations for and restrictions upon us. And, third, when parents come to advanced age, their physical needs or mental incapabilities may so weigh upon us as caretakers that we struggle to maintain proper filial honor.

Sixth

Thou shalt not kill.

God could not have been more direct or clear in His prohibition against murder. Yet self-serving attitudes, twisted thinking, and volcanic emotion combine in an attempt to erase the commandment's application to unborn human beings and to apply it instead to spotted owls, whales, and worms.

Seventh

Thou shalt not commit adultery.

Christian women in our modern era are failing on this point more than ever before. It is our emotional self that is vulnerable, and Satan presents numberless allurements. We know, both intellectually and via a Christian conscience, that God has said "Thou shalt not"; but if emotional hunger becomes great enough, we may fall into the temptation trap the enemy keeps ready. Proverbs 27:7 expresses the core reality:

The full soul loatheth an honeycomb; but to the hungry soul every bitter thing is sweet.

Eighth

> *Thou shalt not steal.*

Mindset plays the lead role in disobedience here. A Christian can conveniently relegate stealing to obvious, reprehensible things like bank robbery or embezzlement. She then can cloak tax-form falsehoods, grocery bill undercharges, and so forth with acceptability. Nor do many of us consider gossip to be what it is: stealing a person's reputation.

Ninth

> *Thou shalt not bear false witness against thy neighbor.*

When we gossip about someone, we not only steal that person's good reputation but we also, in all probability, lie—either firsthand or secondhand (by perpetuating the original falsehood). Again, our attitude toward the sin of lying is a key factor in defying this commandment.

Tenth

> *Thou shalt not covet thy neighbour's house, thou shalt not covet thy neighbour's wife, nor his manservant, nor his maidservant, nor his ox, nor his ass, nor any thing that is thy neighbour's (Exodus 20:2-17).*

God sets forth specifics in His instruction against covetousness, giving wide coverage to others' possessions or circumstances that we might envy. Yet our wrong mental focus and emotional dissatisfaction repeatedly bring disobedience.

Though largely ignored and scorned by modern society, the Ten Commandments continue to stand as God's measuring stick. **It is a measure before which each of us must acknowledge shortfall.**

We born-again Christians, removed by salvation from the *condemnation* of the law, must continue to recognize and obey its *constraining.* The Lord Jesus Christ in His earthly life perfectly fulfilled the law. In that unmarred obedience He demonstrated Himself to be the blessed Lamb without blemish. As His followers, you and I are told that we are to walk as He walked! While that does not mean perfection, it does mean *obedience.*

Our conformity to the law of God has multiple results: First, it pleases the Father:

> And whatsoever we ask, we receive of him,
> because we keep his commandments, and do those
> things that are pleasing in his sight (I John 3:22).

Second, obedience demonstrates that our individual, personal relationship with God is genuine:

> And hereby we do know that we know him, if we
> keep his commandments. He that saith, I know him,
> and keepeth not his commandments, is a liar, and the
> truth is not in him (I John 2:3-4).

Third, obedience is rewarded by God's best for us in every area of life:

> Ye shall walk in all the ways which the Lord your
> God hath commanded you, that ye may live, and that
> it may be well with you, and that ye may prolong
> your days in the land which ye shall possess
> (Deuteronomy 5:33).

*And the Lord commanded us to do all these
statutes, to fear the Lord our God, for our good
always (Deuteronomy 6:24).*

In all, Israel spent a full year encamped at Sinai.
During the final months of their sojourn, they constructed
the tabernacle. Whereas they were traitorous in constructing the golden calf, they were faithful in constructing the
tabernacle.

The final chapters of Exodus, all of Leviticus, and the
early chapters of Numbers present detailed instructions for
Israel's obedient life and service in God's covenant relationship. The principle of sacrifice for sin is pervasive
throughout. In the long months Jehovah held the
Israelites at Sinai, it was as if He underlined and high-
lighted the law He had written in stone. Disobedience at
any point—sin—is serious, and God's holiness demands
that sin be punished. If you and I are to exert consistent
control over our "inner man," and thus direct our "outer
man" into God-pleasing actions, we need to extend our
time at Sinai too.

Only by the shedding of blood could sin be forgiven;
only a substitute *without blemish* could serve in the transaction. The hill of regulation, Sinai, pointed forward through
multiplied hundreds of years to the hill of redemption,
Golgotha. At Sinai God prescribed His system of animal
sacrifices by which sin was forgiven temporally. The first of
those innumerable sacrifices is described in Leviticus 9:1-4:

> *And it came to pass on the eighth day, that Moses
> called Aaron and his sons, and the elders of Israel;
> and he said unto Aaron, Take thee a young calf for a
> sin offering, and a ram for a burnt offering, without*

*blemish, and offer them before the Lord. And unto
the children of Israel thou shalt speak, saying, Take
ye a kid of the goats for a sin offering; and a calf and
a lamb, both of the first year, without blemish, for a
burnt offering; also a bullock and a ram for peace of-
ferings, to sacrifice before the Lord; and a meat offering mingled with oil: for to day the Lord will appear
unto you.*

Throughout the remainder of the Old Testament and
into the New Testament, unimaginable numbers of animals and birds died upon sacrificial altars. The blood of
those innocent substitutes, though collectively it would
have created rivers and lakes, was severely limited in its
effectiveness: blood had to be shed repeatedly, and it provided forgiveness only temporarily.

On Calvary God presented His Son, Jesus Christ, as
the single, unique, and all-sufficient sacrifice by which sin
is forgiven eternally.

*Christ hath redeemed us from the curse of the law,
being made a curse for us: for it is written, Cursed is
every one that hangeth on a tree (Galatians 3:13).*

Each time we look back to Sinai, we should be sharply
rebuked for our false gods, challenged toward greater obedience to the Word, and made to rejoice anew in the dear
Lamb of God, whose death and resurrection perfectly accomplished our salvation.

TEARS IN PARAN

We take up the tale of the wilderness travels again in Numbers 9. It was now the first month of the second year after escaping Egypt:

And the Lord spake unto Moses in the wilderness of Sinai, in the first month of the second year after they were come out of the land of Egypt (Numbers 9:1).

God told Moses that before resuming their journey they were to do two things.

First, the people were to be numbered. This God-ordered census was not just a physical head count. It was, rather, a muster of Israel's fighting men.

I wonder how the *women* might have responded as the counting proceeded. The prospect of warfare is not a thought women relish—particularly those whose own men must be involved. Knowing that each man had a mother, and assuming that each also had a wife, the numbering of 600,000 men fit for battle may well have been accompanied by dread in roughly 1,200,000 women!

Second, Israel was to observe the first Passover—the special ceremony memorializing their escaping the death angel in Egypt. It took place on the fourteenth day of the first month. God prescribed its specific ritual. From that day to this, Jewish people have celebrated their physical deliverance from Egyptian oppressors. Its highlight is the feast known as *Seder*.

On the twentieth day, the great crowd began to move again.

> *And it came to pass on the twentieth day of the second month, in the second year, that the cloud was taken up from off the tabernacle of the testimony. And the children of Israel took their journeys out of the wilderness of Sinai: and the cloud rested in the wilderness of Paran (Numbers 10:11-12).*

They left the wilderness of Sinai, with its drama, its tragedy, and its instruction. They moved on into the wilderness of Paran. Little did they know that sterile expanse of land was to be the scene of their wanderings for the next thirty-eight years! Upon leaving Sinai, the people expected only to pass through that *"great and terrible wilderness"* (Deuteronomy 1:19) as they pressed forward toward Canaan.

The Israelites carried several spiritual treasures with them from their year's sojourn at Sinai. They had the written law of God (specific instructions for life replacing word-of-mouth traditions). They also had the tabernacle (a specific place of worship and Jehovah's earthly dwelling place). And, finally, they had memory of God's demonstrated ability to provide for them.

Entrance to the new wilderness, however, saw the travelers revert to their old attitudes. A mere three days' journey produced ugly complaining:

> *And when the people complained, it displeased*
> *the Lord: and the Lord heard it (Numbers 11:1).*

As before, so now also—remembrance of God's past wonders evaporated in the heat of their present difficulties. The tramp, tramp, tramp of their feet was accompanied by the grumbling of their mouths. Note how God responded:

> *And his anger was kindled; and the fire of the Lord*
> *burnt among them, and consumed them that were in*
> *the uttermost parts of the camp (Numbers 11:1).*

So it was that the first campsite beyond Sinai became a place of sweeping death: God's fire destroyed those at the outer edges of the encampment. When, in answer to Moses' intercessory prayer, the fire stopped, Moses named the camp's edge "Taberah"—which means "a burning." Surely the severity of Jehovah's displeasure over complaining spirits was made plain in that devastation. But the grumbling did not die with the fire-slain offenders. Rather, the people's complaints took on a new dress: tears.

There certainly was cause for Israel's tears: their sinful complaining and God's sweeping purge. Apparently, however, those legitimate sources of sorrow had nothing to do with their weeping tirade. Instead, their tears were all for themselves: self-pity was the motivating factor.

We feminine beings are bent toward the production of tears. Those salty drops may spring to our eyes for any number of reasons, and in any place or at any moment. There are many legitimate, good reasons for tears. Weeping

may indicate a heart agonizing in repentance over its sin.
Tears are a normal response to loss and to pain. Weeping
may speak compassion more eloquently than could words.
And, not unimportantly, tears are a God-given release
mechanism for emotional pressure. We must also admit,
however, that tears can just as surely be deceptive. They
may disguise ulterior motives, appear in order to impress or
manipulate others, or **spring from self-pity.** This final reason was true of Israel, as it often is for you and me.

In this particular wilderness incident, the Bible points
to a certain segment within the throng as the instigators.
They were the "mixed multitude."

An earlier passage, Exodus 12:38, tells us how this
diverse group became part of Israel's wilderness throng as
they left Egypt:

> And a mixed multitude went up also with them;
> and flocks, and herds, even very much cattle.

The exact identity of these people is unknown. But
commentators surmise that they were non-Israelites, perhaps representing a variety of nationalities. Since they are
mentioned in connection with livestock, they may have
been a servant class of people who tended the animals.

Whoever they were, and however valuable they may
have been in providing physical help, these non-Israelites
became a negative spiritual influence:

> And the mixt multitude that was among them fell a
> lusting: and the children of Israel also wept again, and
> said, Who shall give us flesh to eat? (Numbers 11:4).

Although the word "lust" in Scripture often implies a
sexual desire, it actually has a much broader application as

simply a strong desire, a want. Human yearning or desire for something beyond reach can create a straight channel to self-pity. Israel traveled that channel and joined the pity party begun by the mixed multitude that lived among them.

Our mixed multitude doesn't tend sheep or cattle for us, but it nevertheless serves us. They are the unsaved world all around, with whom we mingle daily. Some serve us in the literal, direct sense: plumbers, electricians, waitresses, salespeople, and so forth. But there are also those who serve in a different way: newspaper and magazine editors and writers and TV news people. These Christ-empty individuals, who comprise the majority of earth's population, are ever seeking something to satisfy myriad longings. The whole theme of their lives could well be termed "a lusting." As discontent is reflected in their walk and talk, the pervasiveness and power of that lusting spirit affects us—often far more than we may realize.

Infected by the self-pitying spirit of their mixed multitude, Israel went on to enumerate the things for which they yearned:

> We remember the fish, which we did eat in Egypt freely; the cucumbers, and the melons, and the leeks, and the onions, and the garlick (Numbers 11:5).

And in yearning for those physical things, they claimed an awful spiritual result:

> But now our soul is dried away (Numbers 11:6).

Don't you and I, likewise, find it easy to claim a disaster of *soul* when denied a desire of the *flesh*? Denial of our desire for a new car, bigger house, or expanded wardrobe may send us into weeping over our poor, pathetic state as

God-neglected Christians. Such poor-mouthing is wide-spread, not only among lay believers but among ministry people as well.

As in every other negative attitude, self-pity is a personal choice. The Israelites did not have to be infected by the mixed multitude. We do not have to do so either. Whatever its original source, the only way sorrow for self can take hold on our mind is *our allowing it to do so.*

Self-pity grows as it feeds upon itself. Thus, Israel proceeded to despise what they did have:

> There is nothing at all, beside this manna, before
> our eyes (Numbers 11:6).

The mixed multitude grumbled about the things they lacked; Israel joined in with weeping complaints for onions, leeks, and garlic. They claimed to have starving souls, and they spoke contemptuously of what God supplied. This portion of Scripture paints a vivid picture of self-pity—a sand trap of negative attitudes and down-spiraling emotions. Israel got into their sand trap in the wilderness of Paran. We women slip into it in multiplied places and times, don't we? We create the trap ourselves with self-pity. Once in the trap, it doesn't take long to get deeply chafed with the grit of scorn for God's provision. Let's think further.

In the present day world the WANTS compartment has grown to monstrous size in individuals and in society as a whole. Real need seldom figures into the equation. We daily grow less contented with what we have and more greedy for what we want. In pursuing our wants, things of real value are trampled or kicked aside.

As sad as it is to recognize the disfigurement of people in general, it is worse to see how *Christians* are affected.

Most sobering of all, however, is the inescapable need to *individualize* the issue. We must not ask ourselves, "Do I live lustfully?" but rather "WHY and HOW do I live lustfully?"

WHY do we live lustfully? Beyond the inherent human tendency to lust lies the influence found in Israel's Paran experience: the "strangers" with whom we necessarily move through life. Around us and with us are those who do not know God. Being dead in spirit, they can live only in the flesh; singly and collectively, they who are in the flesh express *self*. In the case of Israel long ago, there was a relatively small segment among them whose self-pity proved infectious. In our case, we Christians walking the narrow way of Scripture obedience are greatly outnumbered by those walking the broad pathway of self-direction. Unless we are constantly on guard, we can be profoundly influenced by their practices and their spirit.

Before we go further, let me emphasize an important point: God did NOT tell Israel, nor does He tell us, to dis-associate from the "mixed multitude." Sadly, there are some individuals and groups of Christians who live and teach isolationism. They withdraw from normal daily contacts with unsaved people, or even from participation in church. By so doing, they disobey the Scripture commands to *"go into all the world,"* to be *"ambassadors for Christ,"* and to be *"not forsaking the assembling of ourselves together."* Demonstrating instead a cave mentality, they retreat, barricading themselves and their families from the world and its influence. The proper balance is found in Jesus' prayer for His disciples:

*I pray not that thou shouldest take them out of
the world, but that thou shouldest keep them from the
evil (John 17:15).*

Israel's problem in Paran was not that they were *with*
the non-Israelites, but that they became *like* them in lust-
ful attitudes. We must walk as faithful witnesses among
those who are unsaved; we must simultaneously resist an
infusion of their spirit.

HOW do we live lustfully? It's really just a matter of
moving from the general to the specific. First our desire
becomes activated, and then it becomes focused. Again,
see Israel at Paran. They were encouraged to desire what
they did not have by the mixed multitude. But notice how
the focus soon narrowed onto specifics.

Perhaps the things for which Israel whined leave us
smiling and smug: leeks, onions, garlic, and cucumbers.
But let's update the list a bit. You and I certainly wouldn't
indulge in self-pity over a lack of cucumbers. But don't we
often wallow in self-pity because we lack a newer car, or a
nicer home, or an upgraded computer, or a position of
greater prominence, or a higher income, or a prettier face,
or nicer hair, or more time with someone we care about, or
greater understanding from others, or a more interesting
daily routine, or a more romantic spouse, or . . . ? And
soon comes the heart wail, "Oohhhh, poor me!" As I interact with women at retreats and seminars, I often hear
them bewail their less-than-satisfactory life circumstances.
After agreeing that there appear to be imperfections at
one or several points, I try to turn the weeper's attention
to the positives of her situation. It is fascinating to watch
as she slowly adjusts her focus from what she *wants* to

what she *has*. Gradually, the "onions and leeks" lose some of their alluring fragrance, and the "manna" becomes cause for gratitude.

God's description of the manna He provided brings a clear, positive picture of what Israel had to be thankful for:

> And the manna was as coriander seed, and the colour thereof as the colour of bdellium. And the people went about, and gathered it, and ground it in mills, or beat it in a mortar, and baked it in pans, and made cakes of it: and the taste of it was as the taste of fresh oil. And when the dew fell upon the camp in the night, the manna fell upon it (Numbers 11:7-9).

Reiteration of details about the manna underlines the fact that what Israel scorned was not just bread—it was God's provision. As I read the passage, my mind goes to my own pity parties, and I ruefully admit similar sin: self-pity leads to disdaining God's gifts!

Israel's pity party spread from person to person, family to family, until it filled the whole encampment.

> Then Moses heard the people weep throughout their families, every man in the door of his tent (Numbers 11:10).

Although the verse specifically mentions men weeping out their woes, in my imagination I can locate the *women* in that scene, can't you? They're inside the tent, sniffling over their lack of garlic, inspiring their children to similar complaints, and thus driving their poor husbands to such distraction that they seek the tent door for a breath of fresh air! Into the once-fresh air goes the vile breath of family-wide . . . then groupwide . . . then nationwide self-pity.

Do you and I camp frequently in Paran's wilderness? What of our home "tent"? What kind of tears are being shed therein? Do they express tenderness of heart and repentance for wrongdoing? Are they wept in legitimate grief and suffering? **Or do they most often express just sorrow for self?**

Part Two

SURVIVING
THE
Wilderness

THE
Wilderness
PERSONALIZED

Blessed is the man whose strength is in thee;
in whose heart are the ways of them.
Who passing through the valley of Baca
make it a well; the rain also filleth the pools.
They go from strength to strength.
Psalm 84:5-7a

PREPARING TO REENTER OUR WILDERNESS

God intended the physical wilderness to end for Israel at Canaan's border. However, despite Caleb and Joshua's wonderful description of Canaan, Israel's "end" point was a *dead end* caused by faithlessness and fear.

Think back over the wilderness campsites in which we've watched Israel. Their attitudes and emotions have varied greatly from place to place. In other words, their inconstancy was their only constancy. If along the wilderness way they had allowed their experiences to strengthen their character and grow their faith, they would have been ready to move on boldly into Canaan. How God's great heart must have grieved to see them as panicky at Canaan's border as they had been at the Red Sea's edge. Listen to the groaning of His heart over theirs (and ours!):

> O that there were such an heart in them, that they would fear me, and keep all my commandments always, that it might be well with them, and with their children for ever! (Deuteronomy 5:29).

Because the Israelites chose fear rather than faith, Jehovah turned them away from Canaan; He sent them back into the wilderness, where they would stay until the doubting, disobedient generation died. But we will leave Israel now rather than return with them into the wilderness for those forty years. Throughout that time they repeated the cycle of learning and forgetting.

Having followed Israel's original trek with studious spiritual intent, let us now minutely examine the pathway for which we are personally accountable. From this point on we will seek to discern, formulate, and present a definitive personal response.

As noted throughout preceding chapters, attitudes and emotions are elusive—mysterious both in their operation and in their effect. There is, however, a means of directing those internal mechanisms: it is our mind. Of its many marvelous functions, none is more important than the will: our choice-determiner. Scripture is rich with God's instructions addressed to our will.

First, our will operates in response to our spiritual allegiance. A pertinent Scripture passage is Deuteronomy 11:26-28. Moses is challenging Israel to choose obedience in the Promised Land rather than to repeat their unfaithfulness of the wilderness:

> *Behold, I set before you this day a blessing and a curse; a blessing, if ye obey the commandment of the Lord your God, which I command you this day: and a curse, if ye will not obey the commandments of the Lord your God, but turn aside out of the way which I command you this day, to go after other gods, which ye have not known.*

Joshua likewise later issued a challenge to Israel,

> *choose you this day whom ye will serve (Joshua
> 24:15).*

Choices—whether in matters large or small—are
strategic decisions that reflect our spiritual allegiance.
Each choice, too, either enhances or detracts from our
spiritual stature and testimony. So God's challenges, those
words spoken by Moses and Joshua, ring down through the
centuries and are applicable to our every day.

Second, our will operates in determining focus:

> *Finally, brethren, whatsoever things are true,
> whatsoever things are honest, whatsoever things are
> just, whatsoever things are pure, whatsoever things
> are lovely, whatsoever things are of good report; if
> there be any virtue, and if there be any praise, think
> on these things (Philippians 4:8).*

God would not have moved the apostle Paul to write
those words if right focus were not possible through choice.
His urging us to focus on right things also infers a choice
against wrong focus.

Mental determination alone, of course, accomplishes
little. How many times do you and I focus upon and will
to do the right thing but never move on into the right action? For instance, I know I should drop an encouraging
note to a sick or downhearted friend, I determine to do it,
but I don't carry through to write and mail the note. The
same principle applies in monitoring our attitudes and
emotions. Each of us probably has a pretty good sense of
where we fail and how we should change in order to please
God and bear a positive testimony before others. But there

is no success until we carry through and implement our intention. Until that happens, the wilderness will triumph; the Wilderness Maker will laugh.

Successful control of our emotions and attitudes begins by assessing our personal readiness. Three factors are involved: physical resources, trigger points, and positive release mechanisms.

Physical Resources

As mentioned in an earlier chapter, the state of our body influences our mental and emotional apparatus. Our human structure was illustrated with interconnected circles. The conjoining areas picture how the physical interacts with the nonphysical in our functioning. It follows, then, that proper stewardship of the body is strategic in monitoring heart and mind. The Christian woman's care of the physical body isn't just a practical consideration; it is also a spiritual obligation:

> *Know ye not that ye are the temple of God, and that the Spirit of God dwelleth in you? If any man defile the temple of God, him shall God destroy; for the temple of God is holy, which temple ye are (I Corinthians 3:16-17).*

We easily recognize that immorality, self-mutilation, and other destructive choices defile the body. However, neglect and unwitting abuse are also destructive. Besides avoiding defilement, we are also called to a higher charge. Our body should be a means of glorifying God:

> *What? know ye not that your body is the temple of the Holy Ghost which is in you, which ye have of*

*God, and ye are not your own? For ye are bought
with a price: therefore glorify God in your body, and in
your spirit, which are God's (I Corinthians 6:19-20).*

God created our body and maintains its life; we are to
be faithful stewards in caring for it. How, then, can we
steward our physical resources both to benefit the Holy
Spirit's temple itself and to contribute positively toward
control of our emotional wilderness?

Guard your limits

Although we women are alike in many ways, our physical temples nevertheless differ greatly. Each of us is an individual created by God:

> *For thou hast possessed my reins: thou hast covered me in my mother's womb. I will praise thee; for I
> am fearfully and wonderfully made: marvellous are
> thy works; and that my soul knoweth right well. My
> substance was not hid from thee, when I was made in
> secret, and curiously wrought in the lowest parts of
> the earth. Thine eyes did see my substance, yet being
> unperfect; and in thy book all my members were written, . . . when as yet there was none of them (Psalm
> 139:13-16).*

Just as the Creator allocates physical characteristics and
abilities, so He also assigns *individual* **physical** *boundaries*.
To ignore or violate those limits defies the Creator's plan
and harms the created vessel. Each of us needs to analyze
our physical limitations honestly—and then honor them.
Although we must not manufacture or magnify limitations,
using them as excuses, we must realize that genuine physical limits are meant to act as regulators.

Both at home and abroad I find an increasing number
of Christian women unnecessarily experiencing internal
wilderness defeats because they violate their external physical boundaries. A physically exhausted missionary falls into
sexual immorality with a native man; her husband necessarily abandons the field; her daughter is devastated in
emotional collapse. Multiple demands so drain a young
Christian school teacher's physical resources that she loses
her vision for student needs, feels frustration in the impos-
sibility of doing everything expected of her. She finally
ends her ministry due to a deep, chemical depression. The
wife of an ever-busy, steadily advancing professional experiences growing civic and social demands versus intensifying
maternal pressures as the children move into their teen
years. Disregarding the fact that she's aging, she pushes herself relentlessly, trying to burn the candle at both ends and
in the middle. As a result, her physical, mental, and emotional resources disintegrate: she walks out; abandonment
and divorce result from her shattered nerves. Added to
those worst-case scenarios are the multiplied "minor" realities of depleted effectiveness and evaporated joy that can
be found in God's women worldwide. An overloaded brain
and over-tired body prevent thorough accomplishment of
duties; exhaustion and stress destroy grins, but they create
grimaces.

No one can accept every opportunity presented. No
one should order her schedule according to someone else's.
Personally, it has taken me too many years to learn to say
no and to make me understand that I lack the physical
stamina of either my mother or my husband—let alone my
several high-energy friends who never seem to tire. Mom
thrived on a full home-and-work schedule into her seven-

ties. My husband charges full speed ahead from early morning until late night. I'm a good way shy of Mother's seventies, but my "thrive" tends more toward "strive," and my attempt to be "charging" with my husband is often done with a limp!

Priorities confusion is also a major culprit in making us women push past physical limitations. Proper prioritizing is less a matter of lists, diagrams, or charts than of maintaining the sense of God's directive interest in our individual life. Our mindset and heart commitment moment by moment should be "What would *You* have me to do, Lord?"

Ephesians 5:15-17 is probably the key Scripture dealing directly with what we call time management:

> See then that ye walk circumspectly, not as fools,
> but as wise, redeeming the time, because the days are
> evil. Wherefore be ye not unwise, but understanding
> what the will of the Lord is.

The passage urges us toward careful stewardship of our time and an overall awareness of responsibilities; it also assures us that God will direct in how we are to fill our moments, days, and years. Personalize the content of the above verse by mentally inserting two words at the end: "for me." Divine scheduling for any one of us will not destroy the body He created and inhabits. Only *human* scheduling does that.

Guard your nutrition

Just as an automobile needs the right kind of fuel, so a human body needs the right kind of food. Perhaps it is time to pause amid ever-busier lives to take a serious look at how we fuel our own and our family members' bodies. There is widespread physical debilitation due to on-the-run, hot-dog-or-pizza sustenance. No domestic science degree is necessary to learn the principles of good nutrition; they are readily available from many sources. A health-food-evangelist approach to life demonstrates spiritual imbalance. However, wise nutrition can make the difference between constricted physical boundaries and expanded ones. Everything we are and all that we have are God's gifts to us. We are to be stewards over those gifts. That means that, as women, our spiritual stewardship should operate in the grocery store and kitchen as definitely and diligently as in the Sunday school room.

Besides general nutrition, we may experience other food-related physical effects. Food allergies, for instance, can have consequences that range from vague (as in occasional sneezing fits) to violent (actually life-threatening). Stimulants such as drinks containing caffeine or chocolate may disturb or shorten sleep time. Christian women probably most often fail in stewarding physical health simply by eating too much. Overeating and overweight subtly but successfully steal optimum physical health; they also mar effective life testimony. God labels overeating "gluttony," and it displeases Him. Conversely, it is harmful to deny our body the food it needs in a misdirected attempt to reconfigure a naturally chunky physique. The extremes of anorexia and bulimia signal serious spiritual and/or emotional problems.

Principles of good nutrition must be applied daily if we are to have healthy, God-honoring selves inside and outside.

Guard your rest

A tired body opens the way for destructive attitudes and wildfire emotions. Yet rare indeed is a modern American woman of any age who is not chronically tired. Let me share by way of example just one precious real-life woman whose life plainly illustrates the point. She is wife to a church-planting pastor (they minister Sundays and midweek in *two* baby churches). She works in order to finance two children in Christian college. She mothers their youngest child, a ten-year-old. She teaches in a Christian school located forty-five minutes from home. She provides the music in both churches. She teaches private piano lessons for ten to fifteen students.

Obviously, those overlapping demands and the overwhelming schedule throw cooking, housekeeping, laundry, ironing, shopping, etc., etc., into an after-hours category—necessarily stretching far into every night. How could this dear woman *not* come to the verge of emotional collapse?

Although the specifics vary, many of us must deal with multiple, overlapping, time-gobbling responsibilities—all of which erode our sleep time. As a result, danger mounts against the place we live: the inner self. Conservation efforts must be mounted.

Each of us needs a certain number of hours' sleep nightly in order to function at full capacity physically, mentally, emotionally, and spiritually. The need varies from individual to individual. Studies reveal serious impairments caused by sleep deprivation. Yet many of us women push on and on, violating our sleep needs. As a result, we perform our duties with unsteady hands, frazzled minds, and roller-coaster moods.

Somewhere, somehow, sleep requirements must be met. The single most effective sleep extension I've ever found is napping. When night hours run late and morning hours early, a daytime nap is vital. That period of rest during the day need not be long; in fact, long naps leave a groggy feeling. But a ten-to-twenty-minute nap refreshes and reenergizes. Following a recent seminar session, a tearful woman approached me. "I know I'd feel better if I could learn to take a short nap. But how can I make myself sleep?" For her—and for you—the answer is, *don't try* to fall asleep. Lie down or get into the most comfortable position possible and simply relax completely, refusing to think of anything. When afternoon coffee break comes, don't opt for the stimulation of caffeine; put your head down on your desk and rest for that ten to fifteen minutes. Your body will profit much more from a rest than it would from a cup of coffee. Some readers will respond, "But if I take time out for a nap, how will I get everything done?" My brief, unequivocal reply is, *"Better!"*

Guard your calendar

Keep track of your menstrual cycle. Otherwise, the emotional struggles so common to certain times of the month can cause unnecessary puzzlement, distress, and defeat in emotions and attitudes. Whenever possible, avoid scheduling tasks that are especially pressured or challenging for those low physical times. It is also wise to educate the men with whom you live about the reality of PMS, as well as about postpartum and menopausal symptoms. As the old saying goes, forewarned is forearmed.

Guard your recreation

While much of life necessarily consists of work, all of it should not. The old saw "All work and no play makes Jack a dull boy" could have the addendum "and Jill a dour girl." Recreation does not demand big, luxurious blocks of time. Back-off moments can be liberally sprinkled throughout our days. For instance,

- let the breakfast dishes soak; join your child in play.

- work a crossword puzzle.

- color a page in a coloring book.

- sit down with the kids at the after-school cookies-and-milk time.

- do a bit of garden: a small section, a window box, a single pot.

- go through a routine of stretches and hops.

- walk around the yard or the block.

- do something on one portion of a craft project.

- take a break from your desk to do head-and-neck rotations.

- stand while you drink your coffee or tea; look out the window.

- gaze at a restful picture.

- read a page of jokes in the *Reader's Digest.*

The benefit is less in what you do at any one time than in the fact that you simply take a break. Loosening the bonds of constant busyness enables us to smell the roses along the path of life instead of crushing them under hurrying feet and getting scratched by the thorns.

Guard your exercise

A well-thought-out, thorough, regular physical exercise routine contributes positively to overall well-being. Exercise used to be a normal part of everyday life: both men and women worked hard. They didn't have our labor-saving devices. Even small tasks used physical energy. Today things are very different both at home and on the job. Because less energy is demanded, less is expended. Our bodies grow slack and weak as a result. The only effective way to counteract the deterioration is with exercise: vigorous exercise that regularly challenges muscles and bones, heart and lungs. Positive results of exercise go far beyond physical maintenance. While it affects the body directly by promoting bone density, muscle strength, flexibility, and aerobic capacity, exercise also indirectly benefits the core self. It's as if physical perspiration saves emotional "sweat" by working off tensions, and stress put on muscles takes that stress off the mind. Cobwebs get cleared from thought processes, and clouds of gloom give way to joy's sunshine. Disciplined, faithful physical exercise also encourages the spiritual discipline needed for regular personal devotions.

Trigger Points

Each of us has certain areas in self and in life that contain land mines to threaten our attitudes and emotions. Obviously, a land mine added to any wilderness area spells trouble. Where the land mines lie and what they do reflect our individualities. Whether the resulting detonations take the form of flying shards of anger, smoke clouds of sour outlook, or craters of discouragement, we obviously need to reduce the negative effects by recognizing their origination: trigger points. A trigger point may lurk in any aspect of our ordinary days.

One thing that very likely serves as a trigger point for you and me as women is the physical condition of our home. As the nester of the human species, woman is strongly influenced by her home environment. At one time or another, most of us suffer the consequences of fast-paced living: unmade beds, stacked-up laundry and ironing, a sink full of dishes, overflowing wastebaskets, numberless other evidences of housekeeping tasks left undone. Those "little" negatives in a house can subtly and silently become emotional land mines, for instance, by

- the arrival of unexpected guests,

- a joking comment made in public by your husband about landslide closets,

- a critical comment or inference by your mother-in-law, or

- a belatedly remembered agreement to host the women's home Bible study—*today*.

There are of course many other places where trigger points may lie. A typical Greenville day of wind-lashed rain serves as one of my personal trigger points. There's only a relatively small detonation, but my attitude's sky takes on a brownish tinge as I go out into the day's activities. A rainy day may not bother you at all; but other things will trigger a "brownout" of attitude. Holiday times, for instance, may mysteriously bring struggles against sadness. Or mindless routine may make you hunger for some outlet for your artistic nature; your emotional atmosphere turns gray. Or perhaps just someone's habitual use of a phrase, facial expression, or vocal tone may spark a resentful attitude. Or heavy traffic sends you into an "I hate the whole world" mindset. Or . . . The list of possibilities could read on and on. It is important to identify specific ones in your life. Much of a military land mine's potential danger lies in the fact that its trigger point is hidden. Locating the trigger can prevent untold harm. The same is true with attitudes and emotions.

What should be done about trigger points? After identifying them, ask God for Scripture that will harmlessly release the trigger. For instance, my blowing-rain-into-brown-attitude trigger gets deactivated through Psalm 135:7—

He bringeth the wind out of his treasuries.

Positive Release Mechanisms

Just as we need to recognize the negatives of trigger points, we also need to recognize and access some positives that are available to help us. I call them release mechanisms: practicalities that defuse potential "bombs" of attitude or emotion.

One of a woman's best—and simplest—mechanisms against runaway emotional moods and rotten attitudes is *tears*. They serve as the universal language of the feminine heart. We want to cry when we're happy. We want to cry when we're sad. We want to cry when we're furious. We want to cry when we're hurt. And after crying, we feel better! It's as if God built into femininity a special pressure-release valve: crying. Many fights, sulks, freeze-outs, flare-ups, depressions, and emotional disasters occur because earlier crying was denied. That awful lump-in-the-throat sensation, if repressed again and again, can grow into an emotional monster.

Again at this point, too, I draw upon personal experience. An intensely private individual, I live an intensely UN-private life. Too often the times I can't cry (public moments) are added to the accumulated times I *won't* cry (private stubbornness), growing larger and larger until the whole awful withholding bursts the dam of self-control. The out-rushing flood is far more hurtful to me and to others than if I'd allowed earlier tears to wash away the smaller troubles. No doubt you have had a comparable experience. So—cry when you need to!

There is a second release mechanism available for our wilderness challenges. This one is less commonly recognized, and thus less effectively used. It is laughter. The Bible makes highly significant statements about laughter. God indicates that an active sense of humor is a nutritional staple for the inner self:

> He that is of a merry heart hath a continual feast (Proverbs 15:15).

Famine comes to the wilderness of attitudes and emotions if we allow life to rob us of the merry heart's abundant supply. The Christian woman whose heart is scantily supplied with merriment is pathetically malnourished. Her gauntness is not only a personal detraction; it is also repulsive to others and unfavorably represents her all-gracious heavenly Father. The unsaved world often turns away from our Lord Jesus because we His followers are stern, unsmiling, and humorless.

God's Word also tells us that a ready sense of humor has curative powers:

A merry heart doeth good like a medicine
(Proverbs 17:22).

In looking back through the years, I can see many experiences demonstrating laughter's medicinal effects. It has acted as iodine on emotion's cactus scratches and as balm for attitude's bruises. There have also been countless times when laughter's medicine even prevented a wilderness struggle. Just recently on a joint speaking trip, my husband and I met with difficulty after difficulty in our travel. One airline transferred us to another because of delayed flights. We missed a major turn after leaving the airport in a rented car. We wandered miles out of our way through a strange town trying to relocate the route. We were stopped by a patrolman for speeding (he was merciful, understanding our plight). We got lost again when almost at our destination. As all the problems followed one upon another, our tension built; I fumed inside a bone-weary body, tempted to tell my husband it was stupid to keep driving back and forth without asking directions. Then all at once the entire scenario snagged my funny bone, and I began to laugh. Instantly, the emotional atmosphere in the car became sunny—despite the fact we were still wandering aimlessly along dark country roads.

Life has confirmed that there really is something funny in every situation, even if the humor lies only in the foibles of our own humanity. Someone has rightly said, "If you can laugh at yourself, you'll never run out of material." She who takes herself too seriously is a crushing bore; worse,

her poorly stocked reactions medicine cabinet exposes her
to unnecessary and intensified suffering from life's hurts.

God bequeathed a highly active sense of humor (probably that should read, *overactive*) to me through my mother.
Helen Callison Peters came from what used to be called
Scots-Irish forebears. Whether that lineage generally is
characteristically jolly or not, humor permeated the
Callison family fabric. Just as there are two *L*s in "Callison,"
my mother exuded two *L*s—love and laughter. Despite difficult life circumstances, throughout all of her active seventy-
plus years, she viewed herself, others, and life itself through
laugh-crinkled eyes.

The moment that most powerfully revealed the blessed
medicinal effect of her gift came at her deathbed. Mother
had a long dying: she lay in a coma from an auto accident
for fifteen months. Because South Carolina is roughly three
thousand miles diagonally across the nation from Washington, I was able to visit only twice before she died. On my
second visit, Mother was observably worse: she was deep in
her comatose state, and her thin, bedsores-tormented little
body was frozen into fetal position. The emotional impact
on those of us around her bed was enormous, and it seemed
at times to be beyond endurance. But suddenly came laughter. Mother had a roommate there in the nursing home—a
tiny old lady whose body was mobile but whose mental
gears were stuck in neutral. At precisely the moment when
I felt my heart must surely break from agony, little Mrs. M.
began to perform. From her side of the room-divider curtain
came mutterings and stirrings. Distracted from our vigil at
Mom's bedside, we three sisters peeked around the edge of
the curtain. There followed an absolutely hilarious scene as
Mrs. M. dressed herself in layer upon layer of clothing from

her closet—all the while carrying on an unbroken mono-
logue of muttering. When her whole closet's contents had
been donned, her clothing-bulged body shuffled awkwardly
to our side of the room—where with immense drama and
earnestness she regaled the air above our heads with wholly
indistinguishable speech. As she shuffled back to her own
side of the curtain, we went into paroxysms of helpless
laughter. Eventually regaining control, I voiced what we
had all experienced in those extraordinary moments: the
blessed *gift* of laughter we had been granted by God through
Mother. And perhaps somewhere far away in the strange,
shadowed land of coma, Mom heard us—and laughed with
and for us.

THE
Wilderness
PRACTICALITIES

How oft did they provoke him in the wilderness,
and grieve him in the desert!
Psalm 78:40

FOCUS ADJUSTMENT

Having checked for overall practical readiness, now let's move on to outline a response procedure that is effective in reclaiming our internal wilderness.

As we walked through the wilderness with Israel of old and noted their attitudes and emotions, what was the single underlying cause of their wrong responses? *Wrong focus.*

Our challenges in attitudes and emotions spring from our focus. I often point out in speaking and teaching, "Where you look determines what you see." Ah, but *activating* that principle when I crash into a cactus of prickly emotions or trip over a jutting rock of harsh attitudes is extremely difficult. The "natural man" focus goes immediately to the scratch or bruise; to the offending object, person, or incident; to the sandstorm's swirling darkness, or . . . anywhere but the direction God would have me look: **up.** Think back briefly over Israel's wilderness trek. Invariably, they failed to focus upward toward Jehovah; thereby, they failed horribly in their attitudes and emotions.

Through the precious blood of Jesus Christ, we are freed from sin's condemnation; our flesh, however, continues in

sin's *contamination*. The upward focus, therefore, is foreign
to our fallen human nature; it comes only via dedication
and diligence. The focus-adjusting project is personal,
private, and tough.

We must first establish the Scripture approach to our
entire wilderness reclamation project. A passage that
clearly speaks to that purpose is II Peter 1:3-8. Let's break
this passage into bite-sized chunks for contemplation.

Verses 3 and 4 give wonderful assurance of God's undertaking and provision for our spiritual strivings:

> *According as his divine power hath given unto us*
> *all things that pertain unto life and godliness*

When God says He equips us in all things for successful spiritual living, He means it. Any unpreparedness or
defeat, therefore, is not His fault; it's ours.

> *Through the knowledge of him that hath called us*
> *to glory and virtue*

Ah, here's the key—and the tough part. We experience spiritual victory in any area only as we know more
and more of our great God.

> *Whereby are given unto us exceeding great and*
> *precious promises*

As we learn of Him, we come to recognize the reality,
dependability, and power of His eternally settled promises.

> *That by these ye might be partakers of the divine*
> *nature, having escaped the corruption that is in the*
> *world through lust.*

The Christian's lifelong struggle between flesh and spirit sees the spirit advance only as we claim God's promised sufficiency. Verses 5 through 8 set forth the immensity of our project and indicate the energetic spirit necessary for its accomplishment:

And beside this,

"This" refers to our salvation. Saving faith is only the starting point; we're not to remain newborn babes, but we must determine to grow.

Giving all diligence

"Diligence" is a nasty word; our knowledge of God and our growing, successful equipping for victory demands hard work and dedicated purpose. We don't grow spiritually through our own means but through diligent intake of the Word. As a baby grows physically through eating to absorb nutrients, our spiritual self grows through absorbing Truth via Bible digestion.

Add to your faith virtue

The first evidence of genuine salvation is a changed self and life. Christian virtue is not a sort of overcoat to be donned on special occasions or for important people. It is integrity: moral excellence infusing our whole being and coloring our entire earthly existence. Virtue is a root characteristic of the born-again believer.

And to virtue knowledge

God's urging is not toward head knowledge as represented by an IQ level or advanced scholastic degrees. Rather, we're to grow in heart knowledge: perception, insight, discrimination, and common sense—all of which combine to direct our life walk in a God-pleasing manner.

To knowledge temperance

Growth in godly wisdom encourages growth in self-discipline. As we comprehend more of our innate weaknesses and temptation's awesome strength, we recognize the need for keeping a tight rein on self.

And to temperance patience

Patience comes to walk and work with self-discipline. Our longsuffering toward people expands, and our ability to endure hard circumstances deepens.

And to patience godliness

I find it fascinating that there are so many aspects that must precede godliness! In other words, true godliness demands tremendous growth. No doubt that's the reason for so much sham "spirituality" permeating our ranks.

And to godliness brotherly kindness

Our treatment of other people is an accurate indicator of genuine godliness. Unkind Christians are infantile believers; yet our churches are full of them. God's unfailing kindness toward us should be mirrored by our kindness to others.

And to brotherly kindness charity

Godly love is the crowning quality toward which we're told to grow. Charity is the wholly infusing, all-encompassing essence of the blessed Holy Spirit's operation within and through us.

*For if these things be in you, and abound, they
make you that ye shall neither be barren nor unfruitful in the knowledge of our Lord Jesus Christ.*

What a list! It powerfully points out the immensity of
our challenge to grow. Read through it again, slowly. Each
trait expresses itself perfectly and completely in Jesus
Christ. By contrast, check the measure of those spiritual
characteristics present within you at this moment. We are
to grow toward Christ; we're to be increasingly like Him.
That fact, of course, infers our constant focus upon Him.
Recognizing the vast distance between what we are now
and what we're called to be, it's no wonder that our internal wilderness finds us more often defeated than victorious.
Yet, this wonderful Scripture passage assures us that if we
will diligently seek to grow, our ever-victorious Savior will
faithfully equip us to be overcomers!

Our wilderness reclamation project will be neither
short nor easy; there may be pain involved. There will
surely be moments of frustration and failure. But we can
trust the entirety of our life way—internal as well as external—to Him, because, remember,

*he knoweth thy walking through this great wilder-
ness (Deuteronomy 2:7).*

Reclamation involves intense effort against wilderness
conditions. The nature of that striving is made clear in the
apostle Paul's reminder to the Corinthian Christians:

*For though we walk in the flesh, we do not war
after the flesh: (for the weapons of our warfare are
not carnal, but mighty through God to the pulling
down of strong holds;) casting down imaginations,*

and every high thing that exalteth itself against the
knowledge of God, and bringing into captivity every
thought to the obedience of Christ (II Corinthians
10:3-5).

The only possible way to bring my internal self (*"every*
thought") into obedient conformity to Christ is to learn of
Christ **by looking at Him.** That growing relational acquaintance is neither an effort of the imagination nor an
ecstatic "spiritual" experience. Rather, we allow the written Word to reveal Him, the Living Word. The starkness
of our internal wilderness becomes painfully evident in
contrast to the Altogether Lovely One, and we are moved
toward change.

Focus adjustment is meant to strip away layers of
neglected self-discipline, habitual thought and behavior,
unrecognized personal patterning, self-deception, and
manipulative motivations. All of those things clearly pro-
claim our earthen bent and fleshly focus.

Focus adjustment as it applies to our emotions and
attitudes is a demanding process that has several parts.

Hold the Lens Steady
EXPLORE THE STIMULUS

When you suddenly realize that you're in the middle of
a negative attitude or an escalating emotion, the whole
thing seems to have slipped up on your blind side. Besides
the difficulty of the experience itself, there is bewilder-
ment at finding yourself struggling again, or so soon, or . . .
Such moments demonstrate our inner self's elusive character; its processes are obscure. The difficulty of the moment
has a jarring effect, and we look for the cause, or stimulus.

The natural human reaction for any of us is to blame something or someone else; we're quick to point at that "reason" for our feelings or thoughts. But such outward-directed attention is merely a shifting of blame. So— **steady the lens.** Aim it straight at yourself.

Scripture urges, *"Take heed to thyself."* In this instance we do so by searching out places where the real cause of turmoil may hide. Ask yourself probing questions.

- Could this mental or emotional bog be fed by something physical—pain, weakness, weariness, medicinal side effects, or menstrual difficulties?

- Have I created or expanded my own problem by holding unrealistic expectations? No person, circumstance, experience, or locale can live up to the beautiful pictures we paint with the brush of human idealism. The difference between our expectation and reality can mean trouble in terms of attitudes and emotions—trouble spelled with a capital "T"!

- Have I been collecting negative thoughts and feelings about this person or circumstance? Such a collection ultimately becomes an internal garbage dump, unhealthy in its contents and giving off toxic fumes.

- Does the frequency or intensity of this mindset or feeling indicate that I have established a reactionary *habit,* making my arrival at this point seem automatic and unavoidable because it comes so quickly?

- Although I'm far into the unlovely attitude now, at what point did I choose a negative first step? Attitudes don't just happen; they are chosen.

⚘ Is this internal state a reflective or redirected ugliness? Many times, difficulty experienced in one area finds outlet in another. For instance, private relational prickles in marriage can motivate a public porcupine spirit toward a happily married friend; pressure on the job may carry over into irritation at home.

Clean the Lens
PROBE YOUR RESPONSE

As we ask God to expose our self-deluded thinking, we may discover surprising contributors to our unspiritual responses. Again, take the questioning approach in your search.

⚘ Am I displaying a reactive pattern carried over from childhood and never outgrown? Home moldings in the area of attitudes and emotional responses are strong and subtle. Probing in this area may reveal surprising and unpleasant realities. If such patterning is discernible, recognize it to be *changeable*. Go to the Old Testament books of I and II Kings, where it is clear that succeeding rulers in Judah and Israel chose to do evil or to do good in the sight of the Lord; heritage and home training did not predetermine their spiritual pathway.

⚘ What is the name for the reaction that claims me right now?

⚘ Is that label accurate? Is it really my thought-slant or feeling? God's evaluation of our self-knowledge is not in the least flattering:

The heart is deceitful above all things, and desperately wicked: who can know it? (Jeremiah 17:9).

*He that trusteth in his own heart is a fool: but
whoso walketh wisely, he shall be delivered (Proverbs
28:26).*

❧ Am I misnaming this state because its true identity
is ugly or because it seems unspiritual in a
Christian woman, wife, mother, or ministry
woman?

❧ Is pride feeding my reaction? When our spirit
fusses, "How dare she say that to me?" it is pride
speaking. We each need to acknowledge that pride
builds its fence around our selves, our doings, and
our children: a fence of barbed wire. Anyone or
anything violating our closely guarded turf courts
at least resentment and at worst retribution in
one form or another. We could avoid or end
uncountable interpersonal hostilities by
acknowledging that, indeed,

*only by pride cometh contention (Proverbs
13.10).*

❧ Is my response proportionate to the stimulus, or
am I exaggerating? We women tend to magnify
life's little negatives. The enlargements invariably
distort outlines and muddy colors.

❧ Am I being manipulative? Manipulation is often
the engine driving female responses. For instance,
I know a number of self-advertised, "sweet,
submissive" Christian wives who actually are their
husbands' puppeteers: they control the strings with
their attitudes and emotions. I also deal with
single women whose constant "problems" actually
are emotional hammerlocks on family and friends.

2. Does my response break the bounds of self-control? A voice that grows loud or high-pitched when responding does not indicate self-control. Scripture tells me to be temperate (self-disciplined) in *all* things.

2. Am I using this incident as an add-on to a list of negatives "proving" that I'm right, or that he, she, or it is wrong?

2. Have I used this incident as a magnet for long-stored resentments elsewhere? Negative thoughts and feelings don't stay neatly in one internal compartment: their foulness readily overflows into other areas.

2. Am I hurting someone by my response? Icy attitudes, condemnatory vocal tones, and sharp words are invisible but hurtful weapons.

Perhaps this is the point at which the typical woman most often loses the wilderness battle. So let's do a bit of extra lens cleaning here.

Our gender-related tendency toward speech can prove enormously harmful. The feminine feeling-into-words reaction violates verse after verse of Scripture warning about the careless tongue.

> Even so the tongue is a little member, and boasteth great things. Behold, how great a matter a little fire kindleth! And the tongue is a fire, a world of iniquity: so is the tongue among our members, that it defileth the whole body, and setteth on fire the course of nature; and it is set on fire of hell (James 3:5-6).

How, exactly, does that "little fire" first lick at the kindling and ultimately destroy whatever lies in its path?

First, the tongue is a fire through its haste:

He that answereth a matter before he heareth it,
it is folly and shame unto him (Proverbs 18:13).
Seest thou a man that is hasty in his words? there
is more hope of a fool than of him (Proverbs 29:20).

Second, the tongue is a fire through overuse:

In the multitude of words there wanteth not sin:
but he that refraineth his lips is wise (Proverbs
10:19).

Third, the tongue is a fire through dishonesty:

Lying lips are abomination unto the Lord: but
they that deal truly are his delight (Proverbs 12:22).

Fourth, the tongue is a fire through carelessness:

The lips of the righteous know what is acceptable:
but the mouth of the wicked speaketh frowardness
(Proverbs 10:32).

Fifth, the tongue is a fire through gossip:

A talebearer revealeth secrets: but he that is of a
faithful spirit concealeth the matter (Proverbs 11:13).

Sixth, the tongue is a fire through cruelty:

There is that speaketh like the piercings of a
sword: but the tongue of the wise is health (Proverbs
12:18).

Seventh, the tongue is a fire through prideful, empty
talk:

A fool hath no delight in understanding, but that his heart may discover [that is, express] itself (Proverbs 18:2).

Whoso boasteth himself of a false gift is like clouds and wind without rain (Proverbs 25:14).

Seest thou a man wise in his own conceit? there is more hope of a fool than of him (Proverbs 26:12).

Eighth, the tongue is a fire through untimeliness:

He that blesseth his friend with a loud voice, rising early in the morning, it shall be counted a curse to him (Proverbs 27:14).

A fool uttereth all his mind: but a wise man keepeth it in till afterwards (Proverbs 29:11).

Redirect the Lens
SEEK A RENEWED MIND/REENERGIZED WILL

Notice, please: this is central to focus adjustment—the all-important pivot point. The lens of our heart and mind is now to be directed *upward.*

But put ye on the Lord Jesus Christ, and make not provision for the flesh, to fulfil the lusts thereof (Romans 13:14).

The first two steps described, if used in their skeletal form and without moving beyond them into Scripture, could actually contribute to defeat. That is, apart from the guidance and control of God's Word, the process could be used (by an ungodly counselor or "help group," for instance) for meaningless exposure of the inner self. Our purpose, however, is neither curiosity satisfaction nor psychological revelation. We who know Christ as Savior must

address core factors of Christian character: its reality and
its growth. We search within ourselves because the Bible
says that God

> desirest truth in the inward parts (Psalm 51:6).

We also have the psalmist David's example; notice
how consistently the "man after God's own heart" monitors his internals—for instance, when he bewails his fail-
ings, pleads forgiveness, or probingly says, "Why art thou
cast down, O my soul?"

So, having honestly explored the stimulus and probed
our response, we stand stripped of pretense, admitting the
unlovely identity and undeniable power of our emotional
experience. Now we turn—turn fully to God, letting the
Living Word work through the written Word. We must
come with no excuses, no hedging. We say with the apostle Paul,

> For I know that in me (that is, in my flesh,)
> dwelleth no good thing: for to will is present with me;
> but how to perform that which is good I find not
> (Romans 7:18).

Our heavenly Father delights to have His emotion-
torn, attitude-battered girl child crawl up into His lap, as
it were, that she may know His quieting. While He comforts, He never coddles. He speaks truth always; our part is
to acknowledge, accept, and act upon His righteous judg-
ments. Thus, having pivoted from considering our way to
contemplating His way, we move ahead.

Accept God's Viewpoint
ACKNOWLEDGE THE SINFUL PORTION

This point, of course, is where the major "ouch!" comes in the process we're pursuing. Sin is a strong, ugly word. Because it is so, we take enormous liberties and we categorize its applications. There wouldn't be a moment's hesitation in our calling fornication, drunkenness, or adultery, sin; they are open, glaring violations of God's law. We're horrified to learn of someone we know being guilty of such things, or even to imagine ourselves so defiled. Those and other gross violations are obvious, exposed to public view. But what of "little" transgressions—gossip, defeatism, faithlessness—do we hold them to be just goofs? Mistakes? Failures? Boo-boos? Slip-ups? They're merely unimportant glitches in our human composition, right? WRONG. They are SIN—sin not of the body, but of the mind and heart. Their seriousness is made inescapable in the psalmist's declaration:

> *Thou hast set our iniquities before thee, our secret sins in the light of thy countenance (Psalm 90:8).*

So, then, humbly acknowledging our SINS committed in the internal wilderness, and realizing that their presence reveals sin's dominion over us, we must repent of our sin and ask God's forgiveness.

> *If we confess our sin, he is faithful and just to forgive us our sins, and to cleanse us from all unrighteousness (I John 1:9).*

> *He that covereth his sins shall not prosper: but*
> *whoso confesseth and forsaketh them shall have mercy*
> *(Proverbs 28:13).*

How tender is God's heart; how marvelous His longsuffering; how wonderful His cleansing of these wilderness-defeated selves. Rising from our knees, we commit not just our general pathway to His guidance, but our every step to be taken along that pathway. Perhaps this time we'll walk a step or two farther than last time before we stumble and fall again. Thanks to the god of this earth, we will never be able to walk perfectly; however, thanks to the God of eternity, we can walk *more successfully* in His sight day by day.

Finally, Give the Whole into God's Hands
EXCHANGE YOUR WEAKNESS FOR HIS STRENGTH

Recognize from the outset of every challenge in emotions and attitudes that in your self there is only helplessness. In Scripture there is hope and help.

> *My soul cleaveth unto the dust: quicken thou me*
> *according to thy word (Psalm 119:25).*

As God forgives again and again in response to our repentance and surrender, we realize how integral our wrongs of mind and heart have become to us. We recognize anew our earthen structure and its lifelong dustiness. With the psalmist, we come to sigh multiple times,

> *Create in me a clean heart, O God; and renew a*
> *right spirit within me (Psalm 51:10).*

Please don't think of the focus adjustment process as "Erase-All." **God nowhere tells us to *eliminate* attitudes**

and emotions. Both are part of our mortal composition; without them, we would be reduced to subhuman levels. The Christian, however, has responsibility to *encompass* emotions and attitudes so that they enhance rather than mar spiritual renovation. Expressions of attitudes and emotions are to be *subservient to spiritual discipline*.

As long as we inhabit these bodies, we will experience fear, disappointment, jealousy, anger, pride, self-pity, and many variations and shades of those and other internal wilderness landscapes. *Experiencing* the gamut is not sinful; *nurturing* and *wrongly expressing* them is. Improvement in our wilderness walk comes millimeter by millimeter. Ever so slowly sinful habits of response can be replaced. Bit by bit, time after time, we choose focus adjustment.

We recognize the challenges and contradictions in our internal landscape; acknowledge our fleshly tendencies, self-protective ploys, and overall weakness; and now come to stand in utter openness before God. *We give Him* the present situation and ourselves in it; we ask Him to be our living Sufficiency.

> *Not that we are sufficient of ourselves to think*
> *any thing as of ourselves; but our sufficiency is of*
> *God (II Corinthians 3:5).*

In presenting these pathetic, unlovely inner selves to God, He is never shocked, surprised, or insensitively aloof.

> *Like as a father pitieth his children, so the Lord*
> *pitieth them that fear him. For he knoweth our frame;*
> *he remembereth that we are dust (Psalm 103:13-14).*

God's pity for our dustiness is wonderfully, tenderly evident in His dealings with us. Our pathetic, ever-failing

humanity finds intimate comprehension and succor in the
Lord Jesus. Surely the experiential understanding of Jesus
Christ is one of our richest spiritual treasures:

> For we have not an high priest which cannot be
> touched with the feeling of our infirmities; but was in
> all points tempted like as we are, yet without sin
> (Hebrews 4:15).

As we stand humbled and grateful for Jesus' identifying
with our human weaknesses, we're reminded that He, too,
like Israel, knew the reality of wilderness. But what great
contrast is evident between them! Whereas Israel walked
in those vast expanses for forty years, failing again and
again, the Lord Jesus walked therein for forty grueling
days, triumphant at every point. Studying Jesus' wilderness
experience as told in the Gospels makes His responses
clear.

- He did not confine His focus to the immediate
  moment.

- He considered the eternal implication of the
  temporal incident.

- He responded to each test with Scripture.

- He resisted Satan's allurements (including
  misapplied Scripture).

Were we to respond similarly when we come to the
challenge points in our wilderness, we and those around us
would be spared a great deal of turmoil and pain.

Though our strivings are fraught with failures, there is
enormous comfort in knowing that the emotions that so
torture and the mental sabotage that so shakes us were

similarly known by Jesus in His incarnate state. And His having experienced the reality *without sin* is further blessing—for *He Himself is our victory:*

> *These things have I spoken unto you, that in me ye might have peace. In the world ye shall have tribulation: but be of good cheer; I have overcome the world (John 16:33).*

The entire process of focus adjustment could be encapsulated in a single verse of Scripture. That particular passage happens to be my life verse: Hebrews 12:2—

> *Looking unto Jesus the author and finisher of our faith; who for the joy that was set before him endured the cross, despising the shame, and is set down at the right hand of the throne of God.*

The opening phrase, *"Looking unto Jesus,"* expresses the core of Christian principle and practice. Each of the three words is rich in meaning.

Looking. That is present tense and indicates continuing action; as is the word, so should be my focus of heart and mind.

Unto. The preposition is far more meaningful than either "at" or "to." There is the sense of a living connection between the one who looks and the object of the look.

Jesus. Oh, blessed Name. He who is the *"Alpha and Omega, the beginning and the ending . . . which is, and which was, and which is to come, the Almighty"* (Revelation 1:8). Rather than being aloof in His majesty, His strength is ever accessible:

The name of the Lord is a strong tower: the right-eous runneth into it, and is safe (Proverbs 18:10).

The world over which Jesus Christ has victory, the world in which He serves as our strong tower, is the *internal* world as well as the external one. So, then, as we go on to consider practical principles and enabling Scripture passages for our wilderness reclamation project, we can know that it is **victory** toward which we move with our triumphant Lord Jesus.

RE-EQUIPPING AND REJOICING

The Wilderness Within is not and was not intended to be a novel—thus, it will close neither with a happily-ever-after tone nor in pessimistic emptiness. Life is not fiction. Instead, my intention has been to share a sort of spiritual travel guide through our wilderness of emotions and attitudes.

Our travels through the ever-challenging landscape can be made less hazardous. *Improved journeying depends upon improved equipping.* She who continues as a heedless, hapless wanderer imperils herself and those around her; she will encounter multiplied difficulties and defeats.

In order to make her way along the wilderness pathway successfully *in the sight of the Lord,* a traveler must be properly prepared. There are three essential items for her survival kit: water, food, and a compass. That strategic supply, however, is neither bulky nor heavy: all three items are bound up in a single entity: God's Word, the Bible.

Think back over the various encampments at which Israel failed. Without exception, *failure to hear and heed God* caused Israel's failure in their thinking, feeling, and

acting. Exactly the same cause and effect operate in our individual lives today as we encamp in various circumstances. So let's examine the equipment God provides for our control of emotions and attitudes.

The Bible as Water

Wilderness characteristics make it unthinkable to enter such a landscape without a sufficient supply of water.

The human body, by its very physical structure, demands consistent intake of liquid. Whatever the basic state of the body, water intake is crucial. In ordinary life situations we're told to drink eight glasses of water daily for optimum health. Strenuous activity causes the body to demand increased intake, and in times of illness, dehydration becomes a major medical concern.

Those physical factors parallel our spiritual need for water. The part of us that is spirit must have consistent, abundant hydration to maintain health.

Intellectually, we understand that physical thirst is best quenched by water. But often our thirst is such that we want something other than water. While working on this chapter, I was given a living illustration. Three of our grandchildren stopped by our house after school one day. As usual, the oldest, Joshua, said he was thirsty and asked for a drink. But when his mother replied, "Yes—you may have water," Joshua said, "oh, then I'm not thirsty." Obviously, he wanted something to drink of his own choosing; something other than the water I gladly would have given him. Typically what Joshua wants to drink is something sweet—juice, lemonade, or soda pop.

We may smile at the ingenuousness of an eleven-year-
old; but don't we Christian women sometimes react similarly in the spiritual sense? That is, in a wilderness
circumstance that makes us need refreshing, we want something other than the water that God supplies. We set about
searching for something to quench our thirst. More often
than not, we go looking for something sweet—the sympa-
thy of a friend, the escapism of a romantic novel or TV
program, pronouncements by a popular psychological counselor. The Word is often our *last* resort, isn't it? Looking
down from above, our heavenly Father states it this way:

> *For my people have committed two evils; they*
> *have forsaken me the fountain of living waters, and*
> *hewed them out cisterns, broken cisterns, that can*
> *hold no water (Jeremiah 2:13).*

There is evidence everywhere that we Christians are
living as parched individuals. Most of us have to admit our
insufficient intake of God's Word; at most, we try to get by
with a sip now and then. But that just isn't enough. It's no
wonder that even ordinary circumstances threaten our emotional control.

When mere sustenance is in question through poor
water intake, what of the really strenuous times along life's
pathway? What of those occasions when we camp at a Red
Sea, a Marah, or a Rephidim? Sustenance and success at
those points demand special, deep draughts of God's Word.
Our soul should say with the psalmist,

> *I stretch forth my hands unto thee: my soul*
> *thirsteth after thee, as a thirsty land (Psalm 143:6).*

Psalm 1 presents a powerful, water-connected image:

> *Blessed is the man that walketh not in the counsel*
> *of the ungodly, nor standeth in the way of sinners,*
> *nor sitteth in the seat of the scornful. But his delight is*
> *in the law of the Lord; and in his law doth he medi-*
> *tate day and night. And he shall be like a tree planted*
> *by the rivers of water, that bringeth forth his fruit in*
> *his season; his leaf also shall not wither; and whatso-*
> *ever he doeth shall prosper (Psalm 1:1-3).*

Do you catch the richness of the word pictures presented here? There is of course that of the flourishing tree, but its *means* of flourishing is the water.

- The water source is *flowing*; an ever-fresh river of supply.

- The water source is not singular, but multiple; it is an abundant supply.

Our heavenly Father indeed *provides* water for our every spiritual need; we simply fail to *partake* of it. Unlike the planted tree in Psalm 1, we're too often tumbleweeds. Doubtless, each Christian woman reading this book owns a Bible—that precious, essential water. But as in the physical wilderness, so it is in the spiritual: its beneficent effects do not come from *carrying* the water but in *consuming* it regularly.

The Bible as Food

During Israel's journey through the wilderness long ago, God provided very special, heaven-sent food. His loving provision did not end with that historical period. Just as surely, He gives the heaven-sent bread of His Word for our soul's daily use. Marvelous reality! Yet how casually we consider that precious gift; how easily we choose to skip meal after meal. Is there any wonder, then, why any encampment circumstance may confound or defeat us, why the most ordinary stretch of wilderness pathway reveals us to be weak and wandering?

Food is essential to human life. Physical health and strength are not self-sustaining. While we Americans are urged to battle overeating and excess weight, other countries' citizens battle on the opposite part of the food supply scale: famine. Reports of scanty daily food intake and pictures of skeletally gaunt children and adults come to us constantly via the communications media. The contrasting effects of food intake are unmistakable. Famine, of course, is a tragedy in every way. Its victims agonize for any mere morsel of food. In the spiritual realm, however, famine is entirely *self-chosen*. The bread is readily available—the extent to which we avail ourselves of it is our responsibility. Are we opting for soul famine?

The physical human body has a built-in, self-protective mechanism: hunger. It makes itself known in infancy and operates throughout life. There is constant, continuing demand for food—the life-sustaining necessity. A marked decrease in appetite warns of illness or even of approaching death. There follows the question—does my spiritual self parallel the physical in a basic, driving need for God's Word? It certainly should. If that yearning is weak or absent, soul health is at stake.

God daily supplied Israel's food in the wilderness; they had nothing to do with its creation. Their part was only to gather and profit from it. Had they not eaten what God gave, they would have become sick and died. Neither can we substitute anything of our own making. Yet how often we try! In essence, self persistently seeks to bake and flavor its own bread. The attempt to do so produces not loaves, but stones—rocks that only add to wilderness difficulties. And when we go along for days without partaking of the blessed bread, severe weakness plagues us in the way.

Why is personal intake of Bible manna so easily neglected? Certainly our innate, prideful sense of self-sufficiency is a factor. Too, Satan works tirelessly to keep us from spiritual nourishment. However, I believe there is also another, less obvious contributor inherent in our makeup: simple human forgetfulness and carelessness toward that which is familiar. Therefore, let's review the character and consumption of God's bread, the Bible.

First, the character and quality of the Bread is *unique.* It is unique in its *authorship.*

> *All scripture is given by inspiration of God, and is profitable for doctrine, for reproof, for correction, for instruction in righteousness (II Timothy 3:16).*
>
> *For the prophecy came not in old time by the will of man: but holy men of God spake as they were moved by the Holy Ghost (II Peter 1:21).*

It is unique in its *eternality.*

> *Heaven and earth shall pass away: but my words shall not pass away (Luke 21:33).*
>
> *For verily I say unto you, Till heaven and earth pass, one jot or one tittle shall in no wise pass from the law, till all be fulfilled (Matthew 5:18).*
>
> *For ever, O Lord, thy word is settled in heaven (Psalm 119:89).*

> *Thy word is true from the beginning: and every*
> *one of thy righteous judgments endureth for ever*
> *(Psalm 119:160).*

It is unique in its vital connection to the Lord Jesus.

> *In the beginning was the Word, and the Word*
> *was with God, and the Word was God (John 1:1).*
> *And the Word was made flesh, and dwelt among*
> *us, (and we beheld his glory, the glory as of the only*
> *begotten of the Father,) full of grace and truth (John*
> *1:14).*
> *And Jesus said unto them, I am the bread of life:*
> *he that cometh to me shall never hunger; and he that*
> *believeth on me shall never thirst (John 6:35).*
> *I am the living bread which came down from*
> *heaven: if any man eat of this bread, he shall live for*
> *ever: and the bread that I will give is my flesh, which*
> *I will give for the life of the world (John 6:51).*

When we study the written Word, we learn of the
Living Word, Jesus Christ. Our eyes don't stop as they encounter words printed on a page; through that page, which
acts like a telescope, they focus upon the Lord Jesus as He is
revealed. We must guard against seeking sustenance from
humanity-designed bread, that is, modernity's presentation
of Jesus: merely human, sweetly tolerant of anyone and anything, emasculated and ineffective. We can learn of Him as
He truly is *only* through His self-revelation, the Bible.

As we know more of the book, we also grow in our relationship to Him. He ever calls us to Himself. His call is
first to salvation; He then calls to growing intimacy and
warmer fellowship with Him:

Come unto me, all ye that labor and are heavy laden, and I will give you rest. Take my yoke upon you, and learn of me; for I am meek and lowly in heart: and ye shall find rest unto your souls. For my yoke is easy, and my burden is light (Matthew 11:28-30).

How wonderfully unique and therefore how wonder-ully sufficient is our heaven-sent bread of the Word.

Second, our consumption of Bible bread and our living 1 its strength are commanded by God.

This book of the law shall not depart out of thy mouth; but thou shalt meditate therein day and night, that thou mayest observe to do according to all that is written therein: for then thou shalt make thy way prosperous, and then thou shalt have good success (Joshua 1:8).

Meditate upon these things; give thyself wholly to them; that thy profiting may appear to all (I Timothy 4:15).

But be ye doers of the word, and not hearers only (James 1:22).

But whoso looketh into the perfect law of liberty, and continueth therein, . . . this man shall be blessed in his deed (James 1:25).

Third, we should have an abiding, deep yearning for 1d delight in consuming God's spiritual manna.

Neither have I gone back from the commandment of his lips; I have esteemed the words of his mouth more than my necessary food (Job 23:12).

> *I rejoice at thy word, as one that findeth great
> spoil (Psalm 119:162).*
> *How sweet are thy words unto my taste! yea,
> sweeter than honey to my mouth (Psalm 119:103).*

When you or I make a trip to an American grocery store for bread, we find an amazing variety from which to choose. Breads cover a wide range from pale stuff of empty calories to dark, rich whole grains. Most people generally opt for the first type.

God's bread, the Bible, is rich and grainy throughout; it is bursting with the nutrients essential for strength, vigor, and effectiveness in spiritual life. While it contains no "white bread" emptiness, we can choose to waste its health-giving qualities. For instance, we might discard the chew-demanding "crusts" of the Old Testament, only occasionally nibble with dainty reluctance in casually chosen passages, or keep the bread close at hand, enjoying its display, but refusing or by-passing its nourishment. Such waste of the bread inevitably impairs spiritual health.

The Bible as Compass

Geographical wilderness presents challenges not only to life sustenance but also to directional accuracy. A compass is an absolute necessity for anyone setting out to successfully navigate its expanses. The same applies for our internal landscape.

Exactly what does a compass do? It indicates true direction at any point. That is, it identifies north, south, east, west, and the combinations thereof.

My husband and I currently drive a car with a compass built into the rearview mirror. It has been a valuable addition to our driving—both in Greenville and away. It has proven particularly helpful to me. Whereas my husband is equipped with a strong natural sense of direction, I'm directionally and geographically handicapped. Whether indoors or out, I live adrift in matters of direction. (While that fact often leaves me frustrated and confused, it keeps my family well supplied with laughter.) The compass in our car, therefore, has been enlightening. After having lived for more than forty years in Greenville, I now find myself exclaiming, "Oh, is THAT the direction this street runs!"

A wilderness area, of course, is much more confusing than any area of town, city, or village where man-made landmarks facilitate movement from place to place, point to point. Without a compass, a wilderness traveler easily becomes confused: nothing in the sparse vegetation distinguishes itself, searching finds no discernible pathway, unfriendly expanses on every side give no clue as to direction. Yet the confusion, wandering, circling, and ultimate defeat can be prevented by using one small item: a compass.

God gives us a sure spiritual compass for life's wilderness both within and without: His Word. It points always to the true north of His perfect, limitless wisdom.

But, like water and bread, a compass must be *used* in order to be effective; otherwise, its vital directional guidance is nullified.

Knowing the unfriendly terrain through which we move internally and externally in this world, our heavenly Father has provided for our successful travels.

Who among us is not familiar with Proverbs 3:5-6?

Trust in the Lord with all thine heart; and lean not unto thine own understanding. In all thy ways acknowledge him, and he shall direct thy paths.

Ah, but familiarity alone really means nothing. Oh, that we each might personally activate both the challenge and the assurance of that passage!

Because I spend a great deal of time traveling on airplanes, I find some aspects of their operation interesting. Pilot friends and my aviation-loving husband have several times talked together about the importance of trusting an airplane's instruments. As flight technology has enabled us to fly faster, farther, and higher, navigational equipment has become increasingly important. Imagine, for instance those flights in which the chosen altitude is so high that there are no helpful landmarks visible below. Or those caught in bad weather, with clouds and rain surrounding the aircraft, and lightning streaking on every side. In either case, only the instruments can accurately determine a safe path or even a true direction. The instruments operate by reckoning from an external source. The human beings in the airplane are clueless because of vision impairment or vertigo.

As in airplanes, so too in individual human beings— the life traveler can find safe routing only by trusting an instrument. That instrument is a compass—the Bible— and it operates on the basis of an outside source: the wisdom of our eternal, triune God.

Survival and Success

Three items are essential for success in the wilderness: water, food, and a compass. But how, exactly, does the Christian woman effectively employ them and apply their benefits to her personal individuality and to her specific, unique wilderness journey? I've found that all the high-sounding concepts and upward-yearning desires coalesce into reality through

Dedication
Diligence
Discipline

DEDICATION is a heart fastening itself in love upon its Lord and Savior. Without dedication, any attempts to focus beyond and above a wilderness locale is simply a mechanical reaction—perhaps better than that of former days, yet essentially self-motivated and self-serving. Psalm 138:2 eloquently expresses dedication to the great I AM:

I will worship toward thy holy temple, and praise thy name for thy lovingkindness and for thy truth: for thou hast magnified thy word above all thy name.

The dedicated heart is a worshipful heart binding itself to the obedience of eternal Truth.

DILIGENCE. Doubtless this discourages many from following through on dedication's desire. Translated into our everyday vernacular, it's a simple but awful little word: WORK. Simple, awful, and little, it can make the bread seem stale, evaporate the water, and fill the compass with sand. Spiritual development would be wonderful if it arrived as some sort of glorious aura and automatically increased in brilliance day by day. But it doesn't happen that way. Remember the phrase used by the apostle Peter: *"giving all diligence."* In other words, we must expend concentrated, consistent effort to cast off our negatives and seek God's positives. The work is done in and through the Word:

Thou hast commanded us to keep thy precepts diligently (Psalm 119:4).

Our humanity inclines us toward laziness. Anything short of diligence, however, results in worsened wilderness

> *I went by the field of the slothful, and by the vineyard of the man void of understanding; and, lo, it was all grown over with thorns, and nettles had covered the face thereof, and the stone wall thereof was broken down. Then I saw, and considered it well: I looked upon it, and received instruction (Proverbs 24:30-32).*

DISCIPLINE is another less-than-favorite concept. Fallen human nature rebels against any attempt to exert control over it. That innate rebellion is famously miniaturized in two-year-olds. Watch a room full of them. You'll see busy, energetic, demanding bundles of SELF in action. Each is his or her own world; if that world is free to do as it wants, all is well. But if anything displeases or depletes it, watch out! Lifelong, self exults in freedom and frets at restriction. It follows, then, that self-discipline is not easily accomplished. Yet we must exercise self-discipline if the bread, water, and compass are to be effective in our wilderness.

> *Know ye not that they which run in a race run all, but one receiveth the prize? So run, that ye may obtain. And every man that striveth for the mastery is temperate in all things. Now they do it to obtain a corruptible crown; but we an incorruptible (I Corinthians 9:24-25).*

As the blessed three pieces of equipment are faithfully used each day, the wilderness traveler experiences her vital assistance:

> Blessed are the undefiled in the way, who walk in
> the law of the Lord. Blessed are they that keep his tes-
> timonies, and that seek him with the whole heart
> (Psalm 119:1-2).
> And thine ears shall hear a word behind thee,
> saying, This is the way, walk ye in it, when ye turn
> to the right hand, and when ye turn to the left (Isaiah
> 30:21).

We must strongly discipline ourselves with regard to
the equipment God provides:

- We must **make ourselves** drink the water deeply
  and often.

- We must **make ourselves** eat the bread regularly
  and thoroughly.

- We must **make ourselves** consult the compass and
  walk accordingly.

Following are some practical suggestions for dedicated,
diligent, and disciplined equipping.

Set a specific daily appointment. "I need to get around to
it" just leaves us at loose ends. The particular time you set
to go aside unto the Lord is your choice. But be sure it's
conducive to heart intake from the Word and heart outflow through prayer. The appointment time varies greatly
from person to person due to our individualities. For instance, our daughter, Roxane, has her devotions just before
bedtime; several of my friends set aside the first moments
after they rise in the morning. Neither works for me: I'm
too sleepy last thing at night and too brain-benumbed first
thing in the morning. However, a morning time segment
after (a) exercise and (b) breakfast, with (c) a second cup

of coffee works perfectly for me. The secret of finding your
own daily meeting time with God isn't found via human
suggestions; it's found by seeking His direction. Only He
has intimate knowledge of your being and your life. He
wants your fellowship. If you, too, yearn for that and ask
Him for it, the Lord will answer your petition. Whatever
may be sacrificed to gain that strategic time apart with
Him will be well worth it.

Choose and use a special location. Habit figures strongly
in human life. Make it work for your spiritual benefit instead of against it. Too, having a special place contributes
to enjoying a special time with the Lord. I hardly ever sit
in my "devotions chair" at any other time; whenever I pass
or notice it during the day, it's as if my heart smiles, recognizing that unique "God-and-I" meeting place.

Check your attitude. Do that each time you approach
your place and time for devotions. Are you coming rever-
ently, thankfully, and joyfully? If not, ask God to change
your heart. That plea, "Lord, change me so I can rightly
meet You," necessarily begins many of my morning devo-
tional times. Life's like that.

Settle in to work. Once-over-lightly reading or mechanical, mind-distracted moments accomplish nothing. The
basic purpose of time spent in the Word is to learn. The
learning is not primarily intellectual or theological; it is
practical. And there will be tests: not in paper and ink,
but in wilderness circumstances. But what a midget mind
I bring, and what a mighty mind has He who speaks!
Recognizing all too well my insufficiency as I come to
God's Word, I've made it a practice to pray Psalm 119:18
as I open the Bible:

Open thou mine eyes, that I may behold won-
drous things out of thy law.

As your eyes move over the printed words, be sure
your heart is focused and really listening to what God has
to say. That's the whole point.

If you need suggestions for a specific Bible study plan,
go to your pastor, Sunday school teacher, or a good
Christian bookstore. There are many resources available.
However, I would underline one very important thing:
whatever "helps" you may use, *keep your focus on the Bible*
itself. It and it alone is God-breathed and flawless.

Finally, let me share my personal pattern, simply to illustrate the kind of "personal tailoring" that makes a devo-
tional plan workable. It has slowly developed over the
years. Necessarily, it's a bit like an accordion—it can be
squeezed or extended as a day's schedule allows:

- Psalm 119:18
- Old Testament history
- Old Testament prophecy
- Gospel/Acts
- Epistle
- Revelation
- Proverbs (according to day's date)
- Psalm

On days when time allows, I read one chapter in each
of the above sections. A tough day when time is limited
may mean only opportunity to read that day's chapter from
Proverbs and one from Psalms. On a day of whatever type,
my dear Author may suddenly stop me with the impact of

a single verse or even a lone word. He holds me there until He has driven home to my heart whatever I particularly need. Oh, how clearly and powerfully He speaks!

Each day as you go to the Bible, remind yourself that in your hand you hold your survival kit. Its contents are essential if you're to traverse the wilderness successfully.

Take in the bread and the water. Do so by stopping at any pertinent passage to "chew" and to "swallow" by meditating, thinking deeply about, and personally applying it.

Use the compass. Memorize verses that give the direction you especially need. But don't stop with memorizing individual verses. Go on to learn complete chapters and even whole books of the Bible. Necessarily, that means frequent periods of concentration and reviewing. Is that an extreme time demand? No—the more often you check the compass, the less danger you face aimless wandering.

Personalize your survival kit. "Write your name" all over it by whatever markings, notations, emblems, or color highlights you find most helpful.

Let your heart verbalize your intake by writing about it in your spiritual journal.

Go on into your prayer time. Confess where and how you've failed to be obedient, ask His forgiveness, and confirm your desire for increased trust in Him and greater conformity to His will. Pray His promise verses back to Him. Present your petitions.

As you leave your strategic place of equipping each day, ask the Lord to keep His Word open in your heart, though you've closed it in your hand. Ask Him for a continuing awareness of His presence; your talking with Him at odd times throughout any day will become as vital to you as it is in that brief set-aside period.

A Final Word

The wilderness within is never going to be a comfortable place. If Israel had felt comfortable in their wilderness, they would not have kept yearning for and moving toward the Promised Land of Canaan. Our struggles, too, encourage us toward heaven's glorious perfection and rest. Our difficulties can likewise keep us constantly reminded of our weakness and of God's greatness. Too, we must remember that unsaved women around us are struggling *alone and unaided*; how we need to point them to the mighty I AM.

The close of this book is bound up in my earnest prayer that we women who truly know Jesus Christ in individual, saving faith will henceforth see our inner self with Scripture-cleansed eyes. May that clear-sightedness make us aware of our daily challenge to pursue the *lifelong wilderness* project toward which God urges us and for which He makes provision. May it be His voice, His words, which remain with us, enabling us to be moving faithfully *through* the ever-threatening wilderness:

> *Grace and peace be multiplied unto you through the knowledge of God, and of Jesus our Lord. According as his divine power hath given unto us all things that pertain unto life and godliness, through the knowledge of him that hath called us to glory and virtue: whereby are given unto us exceeding great and precious promises: that by these ye might be partakers of the divine nature, having escaped the corruption that is in the world through lust. And beside this, giving all diligence, add to your faith virtue; and to virtue knowledge; and to knowledge temperance; and*

*to temperance patience; and to patience godliness;
and to godliness brotherly kindness; and to brotherly
kindness charity. For if these things be in you, and
abound, they make you that ye shall neither be barren
nor unfruitful in the knowledge of our Lord Jesus
Christ (II Peter 1:2-8).*

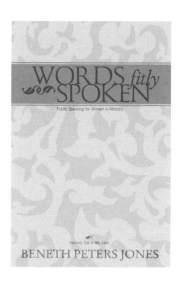

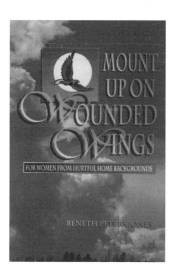